D0393874

Toxic Christianity

Toxic Christianity

Healing the Religious Neurosis

Paul DeBlassie III

CROSSROAD • NEW YORK

1992

The Crossroad Publishing Company
370 Lexington Avenue, New York, NY 10017

Copyright © 1992 by Paul DeBlassie III

Printed in the United States of America

Library of Congress Cataloging-in-Publication Data

DeBlassie, Paul.
    Toxic Christianity : healing the religious neurosis / Paul DeBlassie,
III.
        p. cm.
    ISBN 0-8245-1200-6
    1. Religious addiction—Christianity. 2. Christianity—Controversial
literature. 3. Christian life—1960-   I. Title.
BR114.D43   1992
248.8'6—dc20   92-18475
        CIP

To Paul, Katherine, Maria, and Victoria

Contents

Introduction

Toxicity is a state of soul sickness that develops whenever individual growth and development is thwarted. Christianity becomes toxic as it is rigidly institutionalized. Legalism and the external observances of religion then obtrude on inner transformation that would create independent thinking and creativity. Health of soul requires independence and freedom, not toxic enmeshments with worn-out religious platitudes and legalisms.

Ideally, any religious organization or structure exists to nurture the growth and development of the individual's soul. That is to say, the institution exists for the individual, not the individual for the institution. A healthy religious organization, like a healthy family, encourages individuation and a healthy expression of self.

The life, death, and resurrection of Jesus bequeath to humankind the potential for consciousness. In the words of Irenaeus, "The glory of God in man fully alive." Implicit in this is the fundamental love of God for the human person. Jesus came to impart to the human person the potential for a new way of life — a way of consciousness, growth, and development. The formation of a religious institution, a Christian enterprise, was not His purpose. He did not intend to give us religion and religion more abundantly, but life and life more abundantly. Jesus concerned Himself with human life and human well-being.

Toxicity, especially the religious variety, threatens human well-being. It corrupts the love of self, God, and others; the result is disharmony and misery in daily living. It signals the presence of evil, of willed unconsciousness, not the presence of the Holy Spirit.

In this book you will find expressed ideas about and, most importantly, experiences of Christian toxicity and healing from toxicity. Religious toxicity is a real phenomena that can occur whether the individual is conscious of it or not. In fact toxicity is, by and large, an unconscious process. The person thinks that he or she is quite appropriately religious and God-conscious whereas, in fact, such an individual may be infected with religious toxicity.

My hope is to help to create a greater consciousness of toxicity and interior healing. Only when we become aware that we are ill can we seek healing. In our own day, unbeknownst to us, many of us as Christians suffer from a sickness of soul. Institutional Christianity itself is quite ill. Toxicity runs rampant in contemporary churches and needlessly afflicts the lives of men and women everywhere.

However, my primary concern is not for the institutional church: it is for the individual soul. As the individual discovers healing and transformation, the institutional church may in turn benefit. If so, fine. If not, so be it. What matters most is the heart of the single individual on his or her way to God. Jesus cares most for the single lost sheep, one that is in need of healing from toxicity.

My prayer is that this book would contribute another drop to the consciousness of its readers. Over time, healing emerges as consciousness builds. I am reminded of a story from the Desert Fathers:

> Abba Poemen said: The nature of water is yielding, and that of a stone is hard. Yet, if you hang a bottle filled with water above the stone so that the water drips drop by drop, it will wear a hole in the stone. In the same way the word of God is tender, and our heart is hard. So when people hear the word of God frequently, their hearts are open to the love of God.

We, as Christians, can grow out of toxicity and into life, into the fullness of life that Jesus Himself experienced and desires for us. His word for each of us resounds, "I have come that you may have life and have it to the full."

One

Healing the Pain of Everyday Life

Heartfelt feelings touch the presence of the Living Jesus. All inner healing begins and ends with feelings — encountering God within the soul. As pain and conflicts, emotional and spiritual toxins, steadily make themselves known in and through feelings, then healing is close at hand. Anger, guilt, and fear latently carry the seeds of Divine Grace, as healing springs forth from feelings. In His Own Image, God created us with feelings, feelings to discern pain and presence — His Presence.

Emotional and spiritual toxins interfere with our experience of God's presence in the soul and create oblivion in everyday life. These toxins are those dangerously unhealthy experiences that result from unhealthy inner and outer relationships. A toxic inner relationship would consist of a negative attitude towards oneself that possesses the soul with feelings such as rage, resentment, the will to power, low self-esteem, or a host of other frightful inner devils. Toxic outer relationships, unhealthy emotional and spiritual ties with people, create such discord and chaos in life that toxins can be felt to run rampant in the soul.

The presence of inner toxins is known by feelings of dis-ease on the inside and chaos and confusion on the outside. That is to say, a person lacks inner peace and outer harmony when consumed by toxins. Feelings enable one to discern God's presence and the presence of toxins.

St. Paul in his letter to the Colossians eloquently wrote, "If then you have been raised with Christ, seek the things that are above, where Christ is, seated at the right hand of God. Set your minds on things that are above, not on things that are on earth. For you have died, and your life is hid with Christ in God" (Col 3:1–3).

St. Paul encourages the believer to "set your mind on things that are above"; it is here he makes reference to feelings. A more literal translation would read, "Set your affection on heaven." More simply, the human soul longs to feel the presence of God. More often than not, experiencing a Divine Encounter requires suffering through pain. The cross always precedes the crown.

His presence and personal pain are felt through the faculty of the mind, or what scripture also calls the heart. All intellectual insights, spiritual inspirations, and emotional feelings arise from the heart. Setting our heart heavenward permits God's presence to quicken us with intellectual clarity, to fill us with spiritual inspiration, and to embolden us to live passionately. In this, the soul feels inflamed with the love of God and vitality for everyday life.

A horrifying epidemic plagues modern society. Modern medicine has coined the term "alexithymia" to describe an unemotional and passionless, *toxic*, mode of existence. A patient told his psychologist in a very nonchalant and unfeeling manner that he had been fired from his high-level executive job. The psychologist asked what he was feeling:

"Well, I guess I won't be getting up so early for a while."
Yes, but how do you feel?
"Well, they should have looked at all the facts."
What would you like to say to your boss?
"I'd like my job back because he shouldn't have fired me."
Any dreams lately?
"Yeah, about a week ago, I dreamed I was standing next to a man on the street."
What else happened in the dream?
"The man walked away and I woke up."
Anything else bothering you lately?
"Well, I have these cramps most of the time and my hives are a lot worse."

For people with alexithymia the normal experience of feeling has been choked off. The pain of everyday life has been numbed. Unfortunately, this does not mean that they no longer have problems. Their unconscious and unfelt pain and toxins quite often discover a channel for release in and through physical ailments. Intense emotional energy left unresolved may predispose an individual to various sorts of physical sickness.

The treatment of choice is to assist patients, gradually, to feel. Frequently, as their ability to recognize, tolerate, and verbalize painful feelings increases, so does their physical, emotional, and spiritual well-being. Healing requires feeling. Feeling promotes healing.

When we set our affection on heaven, we entrust God with the full range of our emotions. God has created us with negative feelings and positive feelings. Such natural passions, when deeply and properly understood, heal the toxins of everyday life. Feelings, whether in the form of momentary emotions, unconscious conflicts, or rich spiritual symbolism, when properly understood, always unite the soul with Jesus and create healing, health, and well-being.

A contemplative nun shared with me her story of pain and healing. For many years she faithfully practiced contemplative prayer. During this entire time, she never remembered sensing the presence of God. In her words:

> I knew by faith that He was present. However, I really never felt His presence. All of my feelings were locked up inside of me. This included not only my feelings for other people, but my feelings for God. I couldn't feel God.
>
> Finally, my religious superior confronted me about my lack of emotional expression. She said that I hid behind my smile and that no one really knew me. I agreed with her. I agreed to seek God about the matter. That night I prayed and asked God for His light.
>
> During my chapel time, I was bothered by a peculiar distraction. I tried to rid my mind of the thought. It was a memory of my father, my brother, and me. The more I tried to block out the memory, the more forcefully it emerged. I realized that God might be speaking to me through this apparent distraction.
>
> As I continued to pray and allowed the memory to surface, I remembered my father raging and fitfully beating up my brother. He tore into him with a leather belt. I remembered my brother's blood spattering against the white wall of our living room. This horrifying scene of violence had been engrafted into my soul.
>
> As a young child, I made a decision to never feel strongly again. To show intense emotion, indeed, to feel anything, might mean that I would become hurtful like my father. Maybe I could hurt someone as badly as he had hurt my brother. Never again would I feel. As a young child I decided to lock up my emotions. I covered up my feelings with a smile.
>
> Pain swept over my soul as I relived this memory. I left the chapel and went to my bedroom. For the next three hours, I remained alone with God in prayer. I felt pain, deep pain. For so many years my soul had been heavily laden with this torment. Somehow, in the midst of all this pain, I also felt healing. If I could just hang on, like Jesus hung on the cross, I knew I would make it. Like Jesus on the cross, all I could do was suffer through my recollections and tears. But for once, I was feeling.
>
> At the end of this ordeal, somewhere around 1:30 or 2:00 in the morning, the pain abated. Just as I was drifting off to sleep, I felt

something, something other than pain... I felt God. For the first time in my life, I knew the embrace of His love. In the months to come, I found a psychotherapist to help me work through all of this. The more I grew to be in touch with my feelings, the more in touch I was with God. Now, I feel the touch of God. He loves me.

This feeling of love arose from deep within a faith-filled soul. In this manner, faith and feeling work hand in hand. Faith serves as the basis of spiritual life. Feelings, deeply and properly understood, nourish faith. Without a clear understanding of feelings, one could take depression, for instance, to actually mean that all is lost. Fear could be mistakenly interpreted as a sign that God is no longer present and available for support. These are all misconstruing the truth of feelings.

The proper and deep understanding of emotions always heals and edifies the human heart. Toxic depression, dependent upon the individual circumstances, may in actuality mean that an individual is harboring an enormous burden of unresolved resentment and is in need of working through these negative feelings. Toxic fear, approached with a clear-minded understanding, might indicate the presence of unresolved wounds of rejection and anxiety over intimacy. The real meaning of feelings is usually a deep meaning that can be arrived at most powerfully in the context of a loving and understanding relationship with one who cares.

Sorting through and working out painful feelings loosens and empowers faith. Without the encumbrance of unconscious pathological feelings, the soul flies free to God. Life flows from the heart of Jesus to the human heart when unconscious conflicts are gradually resolved. Healing grace flows like a river in a soul whose feelings flow freely.

In teaching a bible study, my wife, Kathy, noted, "Whatever you don't work out, you take out. The feelings inside of yourself that you are not willing to face and resolve, you take out on other people. Rather than dealing with your anger and taking responsibility for it, you end up blaming and yelling at other people. Feelings that are taken out on other people hurt other people. Feelings that are felt, faced, and worked through are never inflicted on others. As we face inner truth, in the words of St. Paul, 'Christ Who is our life appears.' "

Christ Jesus felt the pain of everyday life. He lived a life of intimate relationships. Besides over a hundred followers and twelve apostles, He knew the intimacy of close friends — Peter, James, John, Martha, Mary, and Lazarus. In particular, He frequented the home of Martha, Mary, and Lazarus. Jesus felt deep affection for close friends, especially for Lazarus.

When Mary, the sister of Lazarus, approached Jesus, she fell at his feet, "Lord, if you had been here, my brother would not have died." Jesus felt deeply moved and sorrowful. "When Jesus saw her weeping, and the Jews who came with her also weeping, He was deeply moved in spirit and troubled; and He said, 'Where have you laid him?' " (Jn 11:33–34). As Jesus approached the tomb of Lazarus, emotion welled up within Him. Making His way through the crowds, He thought of His friend. Grief overcame Him. As the scriptures beautifully record, "Jesus wept" (Jn 11:35).

Jesus, the man from Nazareth, felt grief, the pain of loss. He did not shun this crucible of suffering. He walked straight ahead to the tomb of Lazarus. He lifted His eyes up to heaven and said, "Father, I thank Thee that Thou has heard me. I know that Thou hearest me always, that I have said this on account of the people standing by, that they may believe that Thou didst send me" (Jn 11:41–42).

In the midst of His pain, Jesus turned to the Father and thanked Him. The Father understood and heard Jesus. Out of deep pain came forth the miraculous: "He cried out with a loud voice, 'Lazarus, come out.' The dead man came out, his hands and feet bound with bandages, and his face wrapped with a cloth. Jesus said to them, 'Unbind him, let him go' " (Jn 11:43–44).

Out of deep pain came forth miraculous life. The pain of everyday life, willingly undergone and deeply understood, creates wholeness and new life. Jesus knows the pain of everyday life. Jesus knows that the pain of everyday life leads to unbinding, unwrapping, and unshackling imprisoned hearts. To each person willing to experience and learn from the pain of everyday life, Jesus proclaims to the hosts of heaven: "Unbind him, and let him go."

Healing Anxiety

The Grace of Anxiety

Anxiety, when illuminated and dealt with, bestows grace on the soul. That is to say, this feeling of fearfulness, dread, and at times overwhelming tension, indicates a need for healing. Left unheeded, anxiety becomes toxic and destructive. As one purposefully delves into the interior pain that causes the anxiety, healing and growth result. In this manner, grace pours forth from anxiety.

A dear friend of mine, who is also a psychologist, told me about Sara, a sixty-five-year-old anxiety-ridden woman. For over four years, she felt the crippling effects of severe stress and tension. Every morning, she would awaken with dread gripping at her. She finally decided to seek professional help.

In her first session of psychotherapy, she described her anxiety. For as long as she could remember, inescapable anxiousness tormented her. Together with this, she routinely dreamed about a howling figure — a wolf-like creature that seemed very menacing and threatening. Each time she dreamed about this creature, she woke in a cold sweat, terrified and overcome with anxiety.

"What frightens you about this wolf?" asked my psychologist-friend. She quickly retorted, "He's awful. In my dream, I am always lying in my bed at home and watching him as he stares at me from the other side of the room. He is fully at the other end of the room, yet I am horrified of him. He does not seem like he is going to hurt me; he just looks so frightening."

The psychologist continued, "Why don't we talk with him now and ask him what he wants?" Slowly she closed her eyes and imagined the dream. Slowly, cautiously, but with great fear, she inquired, "Mr. Wolf, what do you want?" She remained motionless and speechless for the next few minutes. Tears streamed down her face.

Finally, the psychologist sensitively asked, "What did the wolf say?" Slowly she opened her tear-filled eyes and admitted, "He said he just wants to cry." With this confession, she sobbed and sobbed.

The tears, the toxins of forty years had been locked away inside of her. Anxiety signals the presence of pain and potential grace. As her tears flowed, her anxiety abated. In the many months to come, she matured and developed emotionally and spiritually. Grace abounded in her soul as she discerned and heeded the prompting of anxiety to journey deep within and therein discover relief and wholeness.

Generally, anxiety surfaces as the result of two types of conflict. On one hand, individuals may flee from facing and resolving hurtful feelings that have been generated interpersonally. That is to say, people hurt people and, consequently, people can heal people. Provided that individuals exercise honesty mixed with sensitivity, heart-to-heart healing can indeed take place. The crucial factors are that hurt feelings are admitted, talked about in an understanding and sensitive manner, and understood.

Frequently, in church settings, people have the tendency to spiritual-ize what is an interpersonal concern. So easily does one turn to God when, in fact, it is one's neighbor that needs to be approached. When people are put off, God is put off — our relationship with God is reflected in our relationship with people. Sensitivity and understanding in human relationships reflects a genuine and deep relationship with God.

Anxiety mounts and irritability sets in whenever people are pushed away for the sake of "turning to God." Of course, God never actually requires such behavior. The spiritual aspect of human suffering should never supercede the need for heart-to-heart understanding. Wherever two people sensitively and genuinely understand and care for each other, God is.

Anxiety also flares up whenever the natural desire for God is thwarted, when people believe that the human realm dominates with its limited intellectual prowess and knowledge. There human ego is seen as all-important, the be all and end all. Without God, humanity eventually runs into a dead end fraught with anxiety.

The actual process of yielding to the Holy necessitates letting go of ego-centered, toxic perspectives with regard to self, others, and life in general. Human knowledge is limited; human perception at times sees only dimly; truth far exceeds the ability of the human mind to comprehend its magnanimity. A humanistic perspective leads eventually to God or, without Him, to a desperate anxiety.

The beginning and end of all things is Jesus — He is the Alpha and Omega. Resisting Him means to resist life in all its facets. Going against the grain of the human soul's hunger for the Holy dooms one to torment and anguish. The step of faith, believing in the Holy without the evidence of tangible proofs and facts, ushers one into a transcendent encounter with Him "in Whom all things hold together." It may last only a moment, but the effects linger for a lifetime, for eternity. Interior fulfillment dissipates toxic anxiety with spiritual strength and exultation: "Thou hast said, 'Seek ye my face.' My heart says to Thee, 'Thy face, Lord, do I seek. Blessed be the Lord! For He has heard the voice of my supplications. The Lord is my strength and my shield; in Him my heart trusts; so I am helped, and my heart exalts, and with my song I give thanks to Him' " (Ps 27:8, Ps 28:6–7).

Theophan, the recluse, wrote of the experience of being delivered out of anxious strivings and into the magnificent presence of Him who is the All in All:

> Here too, the spirit of prayer comes upon a man; but the soul, carried away by it, passes into such a state of contemplation that it

forgets its outer surroundings, ceases to reason, and only contemplates; and it has now power to control itself or to break from this state. You remember how the Holy Fathers write of someone who began to pray before his evening meal and came to himself only next morning. This is the prayer of ravishment or contemplation. With some faces, by light around them, with others by levitation. St. Paul, the Apostle, was in this state when he was carried into Paradise. And the Holy Prophets also were in the same state of ecstasy when the Spirit bore them away.

Gaze and wonder at the great mercy of God towards us sinners: a little effort and how great is the result. Rightly may we say to those who labor: Work on, for what you seek is of true value.

Anxiety, Disease, and Physical Health

Jesus ministers to all those laboring under the weight of anxiety and worry. Anxious feelings burden the soul and potentially afflict the body with torments of various kinds. In the form of worry, anxiety can have devastating consequences on the unaware. But as the light of Jesus is poured into the soul and worries are yielded to Him, health, rather than disease, becomes the basis of everyday life.

St. Peter provides some of the best advice with regard to anxiety: "Bow down, then, before the power of God now, so that He may raise you up in due time; and load all of your burdens on to Him, since He is concerned about you" (1 Pt 5:6–7).

A dis-ease of soul and body creeps into one who approaches life with the motivation of egocentric power. God's way, rather than ego-centered ways, cultivates health and well-being. When you strive after what an egocentric world has to offer, then egocentricity abounds in your life. This almost inevitably leads to an excess of tension, irritability, and ill health.

The body responds favorably to living life "before the power of God." That is to say, the body is meant for God's life and God's life is meant for the body. As you live your life, quietly engaged in the work that God has for you to do in your life, then you are in tune with Him. Since your body was meant to thrive on life, on God, it exudes health whenever you are in harmony and at peace. When God is in control, life flows freely and harmoniously.

To unload our worries on God does not mean that we live a life of idleness and laziness. A lack of worry does not equate with a lack of intensity and discipline. Humbly striving, without strain, to do all that you can do, releases God's power into life's circumstances in a most miraculous way. Even the health of the body favorably responds to responsible yet worry-free living.

A medical study confirms that when people do their utmost, God does His utmost. A research study, conducted at the University of California, San Francisco, and at San Francisco General Hospital, arranged for a group of people scattered throughout the country to pray daily for 192 coronary care unit patients. Another 201 patients in a control group did not receive prayers. Over a ten-month period, the people doing the praying prayed for "beneficial healing and quick recovery" for each person.

The results indicated that the prayed-for subjects had significantly fewer complications while in the coronary care unit. *Eighteen* patients in the control group suffered pulmonary edema while only *six* patients in the prayed-for group suffered from this complication. *Sixteen* patients in the control group required antibiotics while only *three* patients in the prayed-for group required antibiotics.

The medical staff applied themselves diligently to the recuperation and rehabilitation of each patient. This attentiveness combined with a yielding to the healing grace of Providence provided an unobstructed conduit in which prayer and medicine worked hand in hand.

A worry-free approach to life works in much the same manner. Wholehearted trust in God, combined with disciplined work, creates the necessary climate to cultivate the ever-present and ever-ready grace of God. No amount of worry can substitute for hard work. With hard work and a worry-free dependence upon God, health of body, mind, and soul is furthered.

Well-being or ill health can often be fostered by the attitudes of doctors toward their patients. A pessimistic view by a doctor toward his patient's condition often exacerbates already helpless and anxiety-ridden feelings in the patient. Norman Cousins reviewed 300 cases of patients with malignancies whose course rapidly degenerated after the pronouncement of diagnosis. He questioned, "Is it possible that the diagnosis has the effect of...a pronouncement of doom?"

Robert Mendelsohn of the University of Illinois School of Medicine follows this way of thinking: "It's one thing to inform a patient that he or she suffers from a deadly disease and that the magic of the doctor doesn't go far enough to do any good. But it's another thing entirely to tell a patient that the end is inevitable."

He advocates that doctors be honest with their patients with regard to both the diagnosis and the medical findings on the effects that a "fighting" spirit and a positive attitude have on the course of disease. Doctors can inspire patients to adopt attitudes that will activate self-healing systems.

Bernard Lown, a Harvard professor of cardiology, reported that early in his career, a supervising physician was making rounds and examined a middle-aged woman with congestive heart failure and swelling in the ankles from an accumulation of fluid. Her condition required care and attention, but was not considered extremely serious. The supervising physician turned to the medical residents following him and announced, "This woman has TS." No sooner had he said this, than the woman began breathing rapidly, perspiring profusely, and experiencing a quickened pulse of more than 150 beats a minute.

Professor Lown quickly examined her and found that her lungs, which had formerly been clear, had an accumulation of fluid. Her anxiety and upset triggered a horrendous physical reaction that endangered her well-being. When questioned about this matter, she responded that she had heard that she had TS and knew that it meant "terminal situation." Lown immediately reassured her that TS meant "tricuspid stenosis" — a narrowing of the tricuspid heart valve. It was not a terminal situation. Despite his efforts to reassure her, the woman developed massive lung congestion and later died that same day from heart failure. Lown said he would never forget the power of the physician's word.

As King Solomon so aptly wrote: "The tongue has the power of life and death." The tongue, speaking anxiety or ease, encouragement or discouragement, trust or worry, breeds illness or health. Anxiety breeds disease; trust in Jesus breeds well-being.

Holiness — The Cure for Anxiety

The holy apostle St. Paul wrote: "Never worry about anything; but tell God all of your desires of every kind in prayer and petition shot through with gratitude, and the peace of God which is beyond our understanding will guard your hearts and your thoughts in Christ Jesus" (Phil 4:6–7).

Worry potentially destroys interior peace. The ability to never worry about anything permits the sentinel of God's peace to constantly stand guard over the heart. Such an inner tranquility escapes our intellectual comprehension, but can be fully realized in the depths of the heart. In other words, even though God's peace cannot be completely detailed and explained, it can be fully experienced.

Anthony, a man of deep spiritual yearnings, confided that worry had gotten hold of him without his even realizing it. Little by little, he had noticed his spiritual peace decreasing, leaving him open to irritability and interpersonal strife. He prayed for an answer. The answer came while in the depths of sleep, with ego defenses suspended and his innermost heart fully yielded to the One Who held him in the palms of His hands:

At the beginning of the dream, I noticed myself talking with a number of people in my family. These people tend to be preoccupied by minor everyday events. They talk incessantly about sales at one store or another, the sports on television, and the weather. Never does their conversation deepen. A white-haired old man guided me to move away from them. He walked with me into another room. In fact, it seemed as though we entered another home. This home was very large, three stories with intricate carvings on the walls and ceilings. The house felt very Victorian. Its design was rich and intricate in detail. Light flooded the home. It was immense, yet warm and comfortable. We moved quickly to the third story of the home and there found a large foyer. It seemed to be thirty feet by thirty feet. A short semi-circular hallway at the end of the room with white walls curved into a round sanctuary. The sanctuary was large, simple but yet elegant. The whiteness of the walls exuded purity. The oak floors breathed richness and warmth. God was present in this room.

Anthony remarked:

I awoke from this dream realizing its implications. The worries of everyday life, symbolized by the idle chattering of family members at the beginning of the dream, need not captivate me. I found a better and deeper way. Instead of giving in to anxieties and worries, I now feel the grace to move into the depths of my soul. As with the house in my dreams, my inner life is intricate and rich. At its deepest level is a hidden sanctuary. God lives within me in purity, richness, and warmth. I am moving in Him. Since this dream, I have never again been troubled by worry. Grace led me into the heart of God. Holiness cured my worry.

Healing Depression

Just as Jesus beckons all who feel anxious and worried to come unto Him, so, also, He opens His arms to all those troubled by depression.

Feelings of self-doubt, negativism toward self and others, lethargy, and despair characterize the depressed soul. A heavy heart is a depressed heart. Truth, covered up, causes depression. The unbearable weight of hidden-away egocentricities and negativism crashes down upon one who seeks hiding rather than openness, light, and truth. The soul is made for truth and truth for the soul. Without living life with painstaking interior honesty, an individual becomes prey to the gripping force of depression. Thus, depression signals the need for facing and sorting through one's life with all of its attendant sorrows, pains, and unresolved experiences.

Depression urges the soul to live a deeper and more reflective life. Because of this, depression can actually promote personal growth and interior freedom if its message is understood. At the end of the dark tunnel of depression stands the Risen Jesus with open arms and a loving embrace. Indeed, He is present even during the journey through the dark tunnel. But only with sufficient light and truth-facing does the soul recognize Him, the One Who understands and understands deeply.

Depression in Adults

For an adult, the years have a way of storing up a plethora of unresolved emotions. These unresolved conflicts demand attention as is evidenced by symptoms of depression. The heavy heart is a heart weighted down by years of built-up griefs and resentments. For one who is willing to face inner truth, relief and healing are available.

Robert complained of constant sadness and tiredness. He experienced a drastic decrease in appetite, loss of energy, difficulty sleeping, and withdrawal from other people. After sixty-five years of living, Robert finally admitted that he felt depressed.

As we explored his pain, he confessed that his childhood years had been plagued by a lack of affection and love. "My parents just let us kids raise ourselves. I never remember my mother or father telling us that they loved us. My mother never held me. My father never embraced me. I thought everyone was raised this way."

Such a lack of emotional nourishment during his early years left Robert prone to depression. His marital and family relationships were characterized by distance and lack of communication. Once again, he thought this was the norm. "I never really thought about being close to my wife and children. They did their thing and I did my thing. All of a sudden these bad feelings are worse than ever. I finally have to admit that I'm depressed."

After approximately two years of intensive psychotherapy, Robert witnessed a definite life change. He steadily and gradually had grown closer to his wife. Even his children noticed how expressive he was becoming with them. He remarked,

> Relationships have a whole new meaning for me now. When I go out of my way to be close to the people that I love, my soul feels full. Closeness is medicine for my heart. When I feel close to people, I don't feel depressed. For the first time in my life, I feel good, really good.
>
> In a manner of speaking, depression was grace for me. This grace of depression motivated me to get my life together. It told me that something was wrong on the inside of me. I needed to learn about love. Little by little, I grew to be able to feel love. I thank God every day for this grace of depression. Just like I used to feel depressed, I now feel love, full of love and full of God's grace.

The Divine grace of depression thus urges one to discover hidden-away interior truths. Perhaps at a moment of mid-life crisis, when waves of depression batter the human heart, one finally agrees to reflect on the meaning of his or her life. This heavy hand of God nudges one toward growth and development. Properly considered, depression signals not demise but the potential dawn of new life.

Only by surrendering to the presence of the living Jesus within, does healing come. In the words of the psalmist, "For in You, Yahweh, I put my hope, You, Lord my God, will give answer" (Ps 38:150).

Overcoming Childhood Depression

Tommy, a twelve-year-old boy, came home from school quite disgruntled and irritable. His mother quickly asked the reason for his angry attitude. He responded, "Now, you're picking on me too. I just wish everyone would leave me alone." He ran to his bedroom. His mother sensed that he needed time to be alone.

About twenty minutes later, she knocked on his bedroom door and asked if she might enter. His mother knew the importance of respecting children's privacy. With his permission, she entered his room and found him lying on his bed sobbing.

"Would you like to talk about it?" she asked. Tommy nodded affirmatively. Slowly, he confided, "I asked Susan if she would be my friend. Remember, Mom, you said it would be alright if we were sort of special friends, not like going steady or anything, just friends. The whole class found out about us and a couple of guys started making fun of us."

As tears streamed down his face, he continued, "I wish they would just leave us alone. Susan told me at the end of the day that she didn't want to be my special friend anymore. She ran off to the girls' room and cried. I feel horrible. I guess I never should have asked her to be my friend."

Softly, his mother stroked his hair and listened. She offered no advice. She lovingly and quietly understood his anger and pain. After ten or fifteen minutes of pouring out his heart, Tommy looked at his mother and said, "Thanks for being here. I'm sorry about what I said to you earlier. I guess I lumped you in with everybody else. I feel better now that I've got all this off my chest."

His mother ended by warmly expressing her concern and availability to talk more if the need should arise. They embraced with a sense of mutual caring and deepened love.

When anyone feels hurt and misunderstood, depression wells up within. Childhood depression stems from feeling misunderstood and therefore unloved by friends and, most importantly, by family.

Usually sad feelings pass as the child senses caring from another person, hopefully one of his or her parents. If the child feels assaulted by chronic emotional injury through criticism or lack of affection, depression begins to sink deep roots into the soul. Deeply entrenched depression usually requires the in-depth understanding and healing provided in psychotherapy. With passing feelings encountered in day-to-day life, the parent's genuine willingness to avoid pushy advice and, instead, listen quietly as his or her child pours out painful feelings, depression dissipates. A child whose heart is troubled by depression cries for a relationship that will provide healing through caring and understanding.

Jesus and Depression

St. Peter wrote: "As you come to Him, the living stone — rejected by man but chosen by God and precious to Him — you also, like living stones, are being built into a spiritual house to be a holy priesthood, offering spiritual sacrifices acceptable to God through Jesus Christ" (1 Pt 2:4–5).

At the moment of His crucifixion and death, He bore the pain of rejection and depression. Through His experience of depression, there is hope for our experience of depression. Since He has gone before us in all ways, including psychological suffering, we now have hope of being fully understood and fully healed. Jesus of Nazareth knows the way through depression.

Anger: Hungry Love

In one way or another, anger always plays a significant part in depression. In a great many cases, unresolved anger may cause depression. Feelings of resentment, bitterness, and unresolved hostility all cause the soul to be vulnerable to crippling depression. Anger, left unsettled and misunderstood, drives an individual into the depths emotionally, spiritually, and physically.

An angry person is a person who is hungry for love. Love is made for the soul and the soul for love. Empathic and personal understanding convey love. Without such empathy, anger and even hostility can settle into one's life.

If the hostility is intense enough, suicidal thoughts and feelings may emerge. Herein the human heart feels isolated and alone in a cruel world. Other people, and even God, seem hostile and alienating. King David projected his anger onto God: "Oh Lord, do not rebuke me in Your anger or discipline me in Your wrath. For Your arrows have pierced me, and Your hand has come down upon me" (Ps 38:1–2).

During moments of desperation, even God seems far away. Even God seems not to understand but, instead, to inflict anger and rage upon us. It is important to realize that such a conception of God results from the projection of our unresolved hostility onto Him. God is love and only love. He understands, He nurtures, He heals. God understands when no one else seems to understand. God, with the holiness of His understanding experienced by us inwardly, is the great healer of depression.

I remember a young woman walking into my office. She complained of severe depression. No one, especially God, understood or loved her, she felt. Week after week, she attended church and prayed, all without result. Her mannerisms, her tone of voice, and her attitude all seemed hostile.

As I attempted to understand her pain, she candidly shared a dream. She recalled, "I saw a row of trash cans in back of a large hospital. They had black plastic bags in them. The cans seemed to move as though there was life in them. I had this dream last night, the night before our first session. I don't know what to make of it."

I asked this young woman if she felt that the dream, in any way, might have to do with her depression. She adamantly denied any connection. She became defiantly silent. Somehow, I had an intuitive feeling about the meaning of the dream. In a moment of spontaneous insight, I inquired, "When did you have your abortion?" Stunned, she looked at me.

As she sobbed, she remarked, "I never told you I had an abortion. I didn't think that I would have to deal with that in here. I thought it was all over." As we continued, feelings of intense and toxic hatred toward herself emerged. Her depression resulted, at least in part, from the self-loathing that followed her abortion. In the many months to come, we were able to share in the healing light of understanding and grace as we together explored and resolved her feelings of hostility surrounding her abortion and other experiences in her life that led up to this trauma.

At the end of almost eighteen months together, she shared: "For a while I really felt that God had abandoned me. Now I realize that I hated myself so deeply that I had closed myself off to God. He never left me; I left him. With having worked through my anger, I am now free to feel God alive again in my heart."

Grief: Lost Love

As the result of lost love, depression can well up within the soul. The loss of a loved one through death or, in some cases, through prolonged separation can cause an intense emotional apathy. Sadness and lethargy gradually creep in and steal away happiness and contentment.

Depression is different than sadness. Normally, one feels sad about any type of loss. Sadness turns into depression when the grief does not pass. Lingering sadness can soon turn into unrelenting depression.

Many times an individual refuses to feel the sadness of the moment. The tears that should have been wept, the sighs that should have been sighed, and the pain of heart that should have been deeply experienced, all gather force and break down one's emotional doors. Feelings must be felt, either little by little, or through a traumatic breakthrough. Depressive grief signals the onslaught of sad feelings that have been stored up and now demand attention.

A middle-aged housewife found herself weeping for no apparent reason. At first, she tried to dismiss her tears. Soon, she found herself feeling more and more tired and drained. She wanted to flee from people. Even her appetite and sleep were disturbed. She finally admitted that she felt depressed.

One year prior to the onset of her depression, her father died. In her words:

> I never cried at his funeral. I could not understand my reaction. I knew that I loved him and that he loved me. I didn't feel sad. I didn't feel anything at all. Now, I realize why I did not weep. I numbed myself to the pain of losing him. Yes, I loved him... maybe too much. He was my life and my all. I gave more attention to him than I did to my own husband. Now I have to let go of him.

After nine months of intensive psychotherapy, she felt relief from her depression. Her toxic attachment to her father strangled her emotionally. On one level, she knew that he had died, but on another, much deeper level, she would not allow herself to feel the pain of his passing. Her sadness demanded attention. In actuality, it was depression that helped her to come to terms with unresolved feelings toward her father. She now needed to let him go so that she could grow up into her own full womanhood. As she came to terms with her feelings, her depression subsided and emotional health and wholeness began to take root.

Depression and Physical Health

The psalmist declared:

> Yahweh, do not correct me in anger, do not discipline me in wrath. For Your arrows have pierced deep into me, Your hand has pressed down upon me. Your indignation has left no part of me unscathed. My sin has left no health in my bones. My sins stand higher than my head, they weigh on me as an unbearable weight. I have stinking, festering wounds, thanks to my folly. I am twisted and bent double, I spend my days in gloom. (Ps 38:1–6)

Depression struck at the core of the psalmist's physical health. He felt no health in his body. Bent double to the point of physical contortion, he prayed to God for relief. He describes depression as an unbearable weight, and his heavy heart contributed to a pain-stricken body.

Medical research is gradually corroborating this scriptural notion that depression can adversely affect physical health. The Ohio State

College of Medicine has recently published research that suggests that long-held depression can precipitate a physical dysfunction known as Immune System Depression. With this malady, chronically depressed individuals experience constant low energy, an increased susceptibility to colds and viruses, a more-than-average occurrence of various illnesses, including coronary artery disease and certain forms of cancer. Immune System Depression can even usher in premature death — in such cases, the immune system is no longer able to normally ward off pathogenic elements.

But the despair of the psalmist turns to vibrant hope with the resolution of his depression: "I waited, I waited for Yahweh, and He stooped to me and heard my cry for help. He pulled me up from the seething chasm, from the mud of the mire. He set my feet on rock and made my footsteps firm" (Ps 40:1–2).

I remember that during a time of personal distress, I found myself quite susceptible to the flu. For almost two months straight, I felt exhausted and noticed flu-like symptoms. No amount of rest seemed to help. I needed to wait, to listen, and to learn what God had to teach me.

During this time of physical pain, I yielded to God certain of my egocentric desires. I had been involved in a project that I needed to relinquish; for too long I had been pouring energy into it, and all that I could do had been done. The time had come for me to move on to other things, but I wanted to hold on and see things accomplished in my way. My ego-centered determination literally made me sick.

Flat on my back in bed one evening, I told God, "You have it Your way. I will let go of this project. I am exhausted and without energy. I will let go. I have to let go."

The very next day, a dear friend came to me with a healing message. She said:

> Just this morning in prayer, I felt a strong inspiration to intercede for you. As I did, I experienced a faith in my heart that God wanted to heal you and heal you physically. I don't know what has been happening with you spiritually, but I do know that you have needed physical healing. I bring you this rose as a sign of God's healing favor on you.

After several weeks of struggling to regain my health, I was completely restored on the very day of receiving this rose. The heavenly rose was an earthly symbol of divine healing. In my dresser I have wrapped in plastic the petals of that rose. It reminds me always that health of soul and body work hand in glove. As depression of soul is healed, physical health is restored.

Healing Deep Fear

Toxic fear can exert greater power to paralyze the human soul than practically any other emotion. Intense fright can grip at one's daily confidence and threaten to demolish all hope. Under the spell of internal terror, individuals see problems as larger than they really are — a small or middle-sized problem takes on gigantic proportions. Only through deep and steady healing does fear give way to a sense of solid personal confidence.

Jesus is Always Worth It

Tom, a middle-aged banker, approached me with great assurance one evening after a retreat. Exuberantly, he shared:

> I have been prone towards fear. For the longest time I felt like a whipped dog. Problems had gotten the better of me. I really thought I was down and out.
> Finally, I learned about God's solution to the problem. I decided to focus on my faith in Jesus rather than on the heaviness of my problems. I soon learned that I was my own worst enemy. I had what seemed to be an inborn tendency to complain, gripe, and worry about everything under the sun. This trait ran in my family. I remember my mother and grandmother worrying and worrying and worrying. This worry was a symptom of my own long-held fear.
> The more I would worry, the more I would want to control everything around me. I decided that I needed to spend time alone with God everyday. I gave up worrying for one hour a day. I felt like I was entering into a dark tunnel. To let go of control was the ultimate horror for me. During the many months to come, I was fortunate to have a spiritual director who was knowledgeable in psychological matters. He guided me through the dark tunnel of my fear. I was so scared to let go and let God.
> After many months, I came to the end of my tunnel. My anxiety and fear lessened and lessened. Eventually, this fear seemed to dissolve. I emerged from the dark tunnel and found the light of Christ. Discovering Jesus at the end of my dark tunnel of fear was worth it. The more I confronted my fear, the closer I grew

toward God. It was the most terrifying time of my life. But I found out that Jesus, at the end of the tunnel, is always worth it.

Unshakable Trust

The light of God's truth banishes fear. His saving power sears into the depth of human darkness bringing healing of mind, body, and spirit. With wholeness gradually but definitely developing in the soul, fear gradually but definitely decreases. Yahweh saves the fear-ridden and heals all lack of trust.

The inspiration of the psalmist echoes, "Yahweh is my light and my salvation, who should I fear? Yahweh is the fortress of my life, whom should I dread?" (Ps 27:1).

Advancing and increasing fear often feels like great wickedness. Ready to devour the soul, fear can seem to advance and advance, over-riding any last bit of confidence. At times, defeat and doom seem imminent. Fear strikes with only one purpose in mind — to defeat and destroy wholeness. Fear, left in darkness and untruth, may appear victo-rious, as if collapsing under the weight of worry.

In God's company, fear never has the final word. In fact, when inner ghosts of terror raise the loudest ruckus, God is nearest. At a moment when all seems lost, He moves with swiftness to insure the collapse of your innermost fears.

The sacred scriptures confirm: "When the wicked advance against me to eat me up, they, my opponents, my enemies, are the ones who stumble and fall" (Ps 27:2).

The force of fear may retaliate as an army vehemently trying to defend its turf. Around and around worries swirl in the mind. Like a legion of demons they cajole and pick at the human heart. In reality, you are fighting a spiritual war, and the victor receives your soul.

Never, ever need your trust be shaken. With the light of Yahweh's truth and understanding, toxic fear inevitably succumbs. Facing interior truth daily and prayerfully in the presence of God, definitely and delib-erately defeats all fear. In full measure, your trust in God will be restored and never again be shaken in the same manner.

Out of personal experience, the psalmist encourages, "Though an army pitched camp against me, my heart will not fear, though war break out against me, my trust will never be shaken" (Ps 27:3).

Healing the Fearful Faithful

Helen quietly revealed a profound secret:

> For too many years I had been living as a fear-ridden and
> downtrodden Christian. Somehow I never realized it. I believed in
> a black and white Jesus living in a black and white bible preached
> about every Sunday at my black and white church. Everything
> about God was cut and dry. I had God boxed in.
> For fifteen years I suffered at the hands of an abusive husband.
> During an argument, he would strike me with blows that left my
> body black and blue. My pastor stated that marriage was forever
> and, therefore, I was bound to live under this abusive tyranny for
> the rest of my life. Under the threat of hell fire and damnation, I
> remained with a man who refused to seek help for himself or for us.
> In his mind there was no problem. I never wanted to lose God, so I
> stayed with my husband.

As Helen related her story, I felt deep compassion for her years of
pain. As part of the fearful faithful, she perceived God as a black and
white God, a God of do's and don't's, a God who has one set way of
viewing all matters with no regard for the individual plight. This *untruth*
oppressed her soul.

> One day, I just could not take it any longer. Somewhere, deep
> on the inside of me, I believed that God was a loving God who
> understood me. For the sake of my life and the lives of my
> children, I left my husband. I took refuge in a shelter for abused
> women. Now, five years later, I see God in a whole new way.
> Because I left my husband, I also had to leave my church. My
> pastor and the other congregation members ostracized me.
> Frankly, it was the best thing that ever happened to me. I did what
> I had to do in life, and, there, going along with me every step of
> the way, was Jesus.
> My old rigid ways of thinking held on to me so tightly
> because I was a very fearful Christian. Now, I'm free from my
> worries and tensions. God loves me and sees me through everyday.
> My children and I are happy and we're going to make it. I'm free to
> feel God's full love for me and my children because I am free from
> fear.

Facing the Ghost

The ghost of fear must be met straight-on without pause or hesitation. In the church, rigidities, narrow-mindedness, and a black and white approach to God characterize a fear-ridden mind. This mentality has nothing at all to do with the true nature of God, but has only to do with an ego-centered intent to control God and His people.

All light and truth emanate from the Divine. Although God remains ever constant, our understanding of Him should constantly progress. More specifically, our insight into His working in the depth of the soul should broaden and become more acutely clear. Over time, old ways of receiving God and inviting His presence give way to new developments, but in no manner is the canon of scripture or the orthodoxy of faith ever violated. Rather, the word of God is clearly and deeply interpreted within the context of contemporary culture. Jesus becomes more relevant and, therefore, more eminent in the minds of believers.

Thus, a church that is moving toward truth is a church that is moving past fear. Fear dictates a once-and-for-all and never-changing truth. Genuine faith calls forth a progressive understanding of Christian truth as it evolves out of the depths of the soul and the faith-life shared in the Christian community. All that is required is a humble listening to His voice as it unfolds with truth and sets the human heart free from fear.

Honesty is required to face the ghosts of fear. Without a candid admission of fear on the part of the believer, these ghosts run rampant— truth is stifled, and rigidity and severe authoritarianism settle into the church. Vulnerability, a facing of one's fears in the light of Christ, is the beginning of the end of oppression and captivity, of worry, of personal and church-related anxiety, as long as one always remembers the angels' point of view:

> The little angel's face wrinkled in disgust.
> "Do you mean to tell me," he said, "that He stooped so low as to become one of those creeping, crawling creatures on that floating ball?"
> "I do, and I don't think He would like you to call them 'creeping, crawling creatures' in that tone of voice. For, strange as it may seem to us, He loves them. He went down to visit them, to lift them up to become like Him."
> The little angel looked blank. Such a thought was almost beyond his comprehension.

"Close your eyes for a moment," said the senior angel, "and we will go back in what they call time."

While the little angel's eyes were closed and the two of them moved nearer to the spinning ball, it stopped its spinning, spun backward quite fast for a while, and then slowly resumed its usual rotation.

"Now look!" And as the little angel did as he was told, there appeared here and there on the dull surface of the globe, little flashes of light, some merely momentary and some persisting for quite a time.

"Well, what am I seeing now?" queried the little angel.

"You are watching this little world as it was some thousands of years ago," returned his companion. "Every flash and glow of light that you see is something of the Father's knowledge and wisdom breaking into the minds and hearts of people who live upon the earth. Not many people, you see, can hear His voice or understand His ways, even though He is speaking gently and quietly to them all the time."

"Why are they so blind and deaf and stupid?" asked the junior angel rather crossly.

"It is not for us to judge them. We who live in the Splendor have no idea what it is like to live in the dark. We hear the music and the Voice like the sound of many waters every day of our lives, but to them — well, there is much darkness and much noise and much distraction upon the earth. Only a few who are quiet and humble and wise hear His voice."

The God Who Knows Your Name

I know a God who knows your name — His name is Jesus. The nearness and intimacy of knowing that Jesus knows your name soothes the most troubled of souls. The depth of the Christian Gospel proclaims that God knows you and loves you intimately. His singular task is to draw you to Himself, away from fear and toward abandoned immersion in His Divine Love.

The psalmist calls the human heart to an undefiled devotion to the Divine Lover: "One thing I ask of Yahweh, one thing I seek: to dwell in Yahweh's house all the days of my life, to enjoy the sweetness of Yahweh, to seek out His temple" (Ps 27:4).

A fearful soul is an isolated soul, far removed from the sweet savor of God's presence. The greater the inner terror, the more the individual sinks into a sterile isolationism. People are avoided at all costs and God is felt to be far away. In the church, such a person may come across as pious and detached from worldly concern. In reality, this may cloak a well-hidden fear of other people and, in the end, a fear of God Himself.

A regular churchgoer remarked:

> Father Patrick always impressed me as being so holy. He seems to be above it all. I soon noticed, however, that he stayed to himself a great deal, almost too much to himself. I quickly realized that his otherworldliness was a false front that covered up his inability to get along with people. Inside he was a scared and lonely man. He left the parish before I had been able to really extend myself to him. I hope that someday he will find out firsthand that God loves him.

The sweetness of God's love results from a personal encounter with Him Who calls us by name and assuages all fear of being abandoned or unloved by Him. Yahweh's house exudes an ambience of warmth and invitation. All the days of one's life can be spent in the temple of Him Who knows our deepest fears because He knows us deeply, having known our name since before the foundation of the world itself. With the comfort of being known by Yahweh, defenses of isolationism and facades of otherworldliness can drop away. To be lost in His love is to be free from fear and to have found one's true identity as a loved child of God.

The Frozen Heart

A heart riddled with fear is frozen. Emotions, especially love, harden so as to become imperceptible. A frightened person rarely feels the full range of human emotion. Fright dominates one's outlook on the world, other people, and oneself whenever feelings are consistently blunted.

Clinically, these sorts of persons are referred to as schizoid. They appear emotionally cold, detached from human relationships, and too self-contained. Others complain of them as "hard to get to know," or "always in their own world." People are not "let in": intimacy of any sort is shunned.

You never really have the feeling of being able to genuinely relate to a schizoid person. The false self is so dominant that the real heart of the person seems lost. Indeed, because feelings are frozen, the person is frozen. Expressions and behaviors seem stilted and forced. He might do and say all the right things, but one never has the impression of having a heart-to-heart relationship with him. Indeed, the schizoid individual seems incapable of genuine relationships.

Years upon years of interpersonal hurt finally cause enough psychic damage to freeze emotional functioning. Rather than ever be hurt again, schizoid individuals *freeze* their feelings so as not to *feel* their feelings. This protects them from feeling emotionally hurt. Unfortunately, they also sacrifice the experience of joy, love, and wonder. But when one feeling is forsaken, all feelings are forsaken. The schizoid person lives in a sterile world, cut off from warm, human relationships and closeness with God.

God Knows My Name

At the end of a particular week, I found myself thoroughly tired and exhausted. During the course of the previous six days, I had seen a full load of patients, preached a retreat, given two bible studies and, all the while, continued a disciplined course of writing. Needless to say, I felt quite spent.

After Sunday liturgy, someone approached me and commented:

> I heard about the retreat you preached this past weekend. It's too bad that those ten or twelve people complained so much. Rather than learning about the inner experience of Jesus, they wanted a psychologist to help them with time management so that they could work on various parish activities more efficiently. They also thought that hearing about training and communication skills would have enabled them to be more productive during parish council meetings. They wanted the outer stuff more than the inner stuff.

These comments left me devastated. I had poured out my heart, and in my weariness, I thought all I received in return was criticism. Depressing thoughts multiplied in my mind: "No one appreciates my work. All the church ever does is tell me what's wrong, never what's right."

Suddenly very destructive thoughts entered my mind: "You are not loved by the church. God's people only use you for the blessing they receive from you. If they feel no blessing, they toss you to the side and forget about you. They use you. God uses you. God does not love you; He does not even know your name."

For three days these despairing thoughts pressed upon me, and no amount of prayer or personal soul-searching brought relief. Finally, one afternoon, while in my study for a time of reflection and prayer, I confided to Jesus, "I'm hurting. I feel all alone. I feel unloved by your people and by You. All I can do is sit here in Your presence, no longer trying to escape from my feelings of being unloved. I sit here and hope that You understand."

I reached for my Bible and opened to Psalm 27. My eyes fell on verse 4. Over and over again I read the verse. My desolation felt filled by grace as I prayed: "One thing I ask of You, Yahweh, one thing I seek: to dwell in Your house, Yahweh, all the days of my life, to enjoy the sweetness of You, Yahweh, to seek out Your temple."

I closed my eyes, my soul imbued with His graciousness. With His voiceless voice, He spoke, "I love you. I am pleased with your work for Me. I know your name. You are Paul. You are My Paul. And I love You."

With His words satisfying my interior hunger, I once again reached for the sacred scriptures and randomly opened to Revelations 3: "Anyone who proves victorious will be dressed, like these, in white robes; and I shall not blot that name out of the book of life, but acknowledge it in the presence of My father and His angels."

I know a God Who knows my name.

I know a God Who knows your name.

Fears Forever Faded

> Lost in His love,
> Fears forever faded,
> My scars for His Joy
> I have traded.

The love of God fades the deepest of fears. To be fully lost in Divine Love means to be fully found, personally and spiritually. The ultimate fear of dangling abandoned in oblivion, without any sense of love or being loved, pales as the living presence of Jesus Christ shines brighter and brighter within the heart. Ultimately, human love can only prepare the soul for such a divine encounter; it can never fully satisfy the heart's craving for the cessation of all fears and the fulfillment of all yearnings for love. In Him, and in His love alone, fear dissipates and is finally healed.

The scars of fear are frequently quite obvious and unavoidable. Intense and chronic fear may precipitate a psychosis — a break with reality. Individuals suffering the trauma of schizophrenia, manic depression, or other psychoses, know firsthand the consequences of profound and unresolved fear. No longer are they able to cope with day-to-day life. They retreat into a world all their own, a world designed to shelter them from haranguing people who inflict ungodly pain. Psychosis is, in the end, their best effort to go on living. It is true that they no longer function in "normal" reality, that they have retreated into a sanctuary of sorts, but it has been their desperate attempt to cope, perhaps the last option for some.

I believe that God understands the pain of psychoses. He communicates healing through psychotherapy, medication, and perhaps even hospitalization. All of this He does so that one day the fear-ridden soul, troubled by psychosis, will have experienced enough human care and love that an encounter with the love of God will not only be possible, but inevitable.

To trade the human scar of fear for His love and joy is our ultimate task. By His death and resurrection, we have been healed. The process of growth toward fullness of healing, deliverance from fear, slowly but definitely transpires in the human heart that seeks truth and only truth: His truth. Jesus sets us free — free from the bondage of toxic fear.

CONCLUSION
Toxic Pain in Feelings and Relationships

Psychological toxicity is an experiential fact. People feel ill on the inside when feelings and relationships are not in order. That is to say, toxicity, rather than well-being, cripples souls that run counter to healthy living. New consciousness with regard to personal feelings and long-held relationships is the antidote to toxicity.

The Purgation of Toxic Feelings

Toxic feelings in all their various forms (rage, depression, unresolved grief, unrelenting anxiety, etc.) bid the individual to seek the light of consciousness, the truth that these feelings must convey. In order to arrive at this point, the feelings must be felt. One cannot read a textbook with regard to healing the soul and expect to be personally healed himself or herself. The journey must be undergone firsthand, personally and painfully experienced.

To feel one's own feelings is the first step toward health. Toxicity results from damming up emotions, not allowing them to be consciously experienced or expressed. One then feels out of sorts and ill at ease.

One man recalled:

> When I first began to feel my long-repressed feelings, I would sometimes waken in the middle of the night in a cold sweat. At times, during the day, I would feel hot flashes throughout my body. I would perspire and, at times, even tremble. Toxins were being released from my system. My inner pain, the poison on the inside of me, affected even my body. I literally sweated the toxins out of me.

Frequently, I have found that toxins are felt in this visceral way. Emotional pain can be felt and released in a very physical way. The flip side of this suggests that keeping toxins within the system produces severe stress on the body. Physical ailments can actually result from anxiety in living. Emotional toxins reach such intensity that the body breaks down.

All authentic and depth psychologies and theologies must lead one to the experience, eventually, of feeling. Human growth calls for intimate encounters with other human beings and with God. Only therein does a person live deeply in his or her own soul. Without good relationships with God and other people, one can be said to have lost his or her soul. Studies in psychology and theology, when truly in accord with both nature and grace, lead the individual into soul, and therefore into God.

Often a mere intellectual understanding of psychology and theology attempts to pass for true understanding, when in reality, purely intellectual understandings are too remote, sterile, and lifeless. A detached observer can never fully penetrate the deeper mysteries of life. Feelings, understood and followed, lead the way into both purgation and salvation.

Once the purgation of toxic feelings has been suffered, new life abounds. The world appears new, fresh. The pain of purgation seems to have lasted only a short while. Often, after a couple of years of intensive psychotherapy, as the soul finally comes to the light at the end of a very dark tunnel, patients reflect: "Now as I look back, it all seems to have happened so quickly. The days and weeks seemed, at times, to drag painfully on. But, as I continued on the path, the months and years now seem to have flown by. Everything feels new. I feel born again."

The Russian classic *The Way of a Pilgrim* describes the heartfelt spiritual awakening of a devoted pilgrim: "The whole outside world...seemed to me full of charm and delight. Everything drew me to love and thank God: people, trees, plants, animals. I saw them all as my kinsfolk, I found in all of them the magic of the name of Jesus."

Father Thomas was a very prayerful and devout Catholic cleric. However, he had grown increasingly troubled by his temper. Now, with even minor provocation, he exploded in fits of rage. Parishioners had complained to the chancery office. The bishop asked Father Tom to obtain professional help immediately.

Father Tom appeared to me to be an earnest man. However, his Germanic background and religious formation colluded to conspire against healthy living. His upbringing taught him to suppress emotions. The seminary strictly guided him to avoid "particular friendships," feelings of intimacy with others, and heartfelt emotional vulnerability. And always, practically at all times, he seemed to be the perfect priest. His explosive anger, however, betrayed an unsatisfied soul.

> I tried so hard, for so long, not to feel. I considered myself to be a man of steel. I did not allow myself to feel the pain that comes with day-to-day living. I was above it all, or so I thought.
>
> When my perfect composure had been disturbed because of one thing or another in the parish, I could easily escape into a false euphoria. I enjoyed scotch. I enjoyed drinking. At first, one or two drinks a day, soon, it became three or four drinks. Now, by noontime, I'm drinking. Scotch keeps me company through the evening. I feel empty, isolated, and all alone.

As I came to realize, Father Tom felt little support in his personal life. The bishop and chancery office represented a cold bureaucracy that cared little for his personal plight. The parishioners were all right as long as he was their "holy father." He could not be human. They expected him to be a walking saint, devoid of human passion and pain. It finally got the best of him and explosive rage was the result.

After many months of psychotherapy and attendance at AA meetings, he began to feel. For so long, his emotions had been numbed by alcohol. He had forgotten what it was like to experience pain and consolation, sadness and joy, loneliness and love. As we suffered together the purging of long-held bitterness and fears of various sorts, he started to become more stable and at ease. He remarked:

> Feeling is so hard at times. But if I block out bad feelings, I also block out good feelings. Even though it's the hardest thing I've ever done, or at least that's the way I feel right now, I can't turn back. I want to find and feel all of my pain. With every bit of pain, I am also finding growth and joy. When I find my feelings, I find me. As I am finding myself, I am discovering God. He is in me. Finally, I see it, He is in me.

Thus, the purgation of emotional toxins requires feeling and, gradually, disposes the soul toward an encounter with God. Arthur, a middle-aged Catholic layman, confided:

> I thought I was above feeling false guilt in my spiritual life. Intellectually, I knew that God loved me. I knew that His love for me was unconditional. However, I was unaware of the fact that guilt still motivated me.
>
> Sometimes on particular holy days in the Catholic Church when Mass attendance is required, I would be unable to attend. I noticed that I felt ill at ease during the day. It became clear to me that I was feeling guilty, a false guilt. I had legitimate reasons for being unable to attend services. Yet, somewhere on the inside of me, I wondered if God was judging and condemning me. Many times I would feel a sense of melancholia and agitation for the next few days.
>
> Once I understood that this guilt was false guilt, I was able to allow myself to feel my feelings, process them out of me, and return to a centeredness on God. There was no reason to belabor the issue or flagellate myself. False guilt is a form of guilt that needs to be worked through.

Arthur insightfully understood the meaning of his toxic guilt. He could not will himself not to feel it. No amount of conscious deliberation would change this feeling. It merely was. It existed. It needed to be felt, understood, and processed out of his system. In this way, he knew full healing from toxic guilt.

Toxic Feelings and Meaning

All toxic feelings carry the seed of meaning. That is to say, toxic emotions permit greater individual growth and development as their message is understood. They afford one the opportunity to develop new insights and consciousness with regard to one's personal and interpersonal life.

The discovery of meaning in toxic feelings calls one to an understanding that all feelings have their purpose. The ways in which we are short-sighted, underdeveloped, and psychically out of balance, are all revealed in and through toxic feelings. They point the way to new developments and greater inner opportunity for health and interior freedom.

In the end, this causes life to be experienced in a richer and fuller manner. One patient movingly conveyed:

> I feel like I'm born again. For the first time my life feels real. Before this, I related to people as though they were cardboard objects. Now I feel like a whole person and I am relating to others as whole people. I look around me, in the world, and see colors that I never saw quite so clearly. The sky is blue, really blue. Grass is green, a soothing green. The brown earth looks so rich. Suffering through my painful feelings opened up a whole new world of meaning, purpose, and greater consciousness.

Coming into new consciousness requires not only the suffering through of purgation and the discovery of meaning, but concomitant with these, the naming and exorcising of inner devils and, most assuredly, the dawning of the Divine within. God's presence in the soul, felt in and through the exploration of hidden potentialities, must be entered into during the process of soul-making.

Greater meaning in life transports one into the realm of the Divine. That which was thought to be so evil and monstrous now holds great meaning and new energy for living. As darkness is suffered through and understood, light emerges. A person notices a new enthusiasm for previously hidden away interests and creative endeavors. An applied creative investment in life surges forth from one who walks along the inner way. Toxicity gives way to creativity. That which once threatened death now brims over with life. The neurotic pain of everyday life has been transformed into a unique way of expressing oneself in the world.

Carolyn, a middle-aged university professor, waged an intense battle with neurotic anxiety. For many years she awakened in the morning fraught with tension. Anything other than the most routine tasks greatly troubled her. She felt alone and isolated, with no one to understand or care for her.

After approximately two years of intensive psychotherapy, the demon of anxiety had been exorcised. The energy that had formerly been spent on fretting and worrying now found a new channel for release. Her eyes were opened up to the world of people. She gradually learned the art of friendship, the intimate caring for others.

Carolyn's life was transformed because of her willingness to face and deal with the inner devil of anxiety. This dark energy, during the process of working through psychotherapy, quietly revealed a hidden capacity for intimacy. This denied part of herself had been striking out at her consciousness in the form of anxiety. Behind the anxiety lay hidden the wondrous opportunity for relationship building.

Neurosis is always a blessing in disguise. The toxic pain grabs our attention. It calls for consciousness, for a new understanding of feelings, and therefore a new understanding of life. Divine grace always emerges out of the rubble of our inner aches and pains as we perseveringly, step by step, seek greater personal light and understanding of our feelings in our everyday life.

Two

The Voiceless Voice

Praise the Lord. Praise the Lord, oh my soul. I will praise the Lord all my life; I will sing praise to my God as long as I live. (Ps 46:1–2)

Inherently the soul longs for prayerful union with God — an experience of the sacred satisfies the soul's hunger for the Divine. Without intimate communion with Jesus, the soul eventually erodes away because of toxic despair. Steady fulfillment during one's lifetime can be attained via the continual moment-by-moment seeking of God from the depths of one's being.

A heartfelt exchange between God and the human soul comes about through mutual listening. Thus, prayer means not only that you communicate with God, but that God communicates with you. His voice can be heard in your heart if you but realize that He can and will speak to you. Your soul has the necessary faculties to hear His voice. All that is required is a simple willingness to attend to the possibility that He, at any particular moment, would like to speak with you.

You may feel His voice as an unexpected inspiration; it may come as a thought that cannot be shaken. In dreams, visions, images, and symbols, He speaks. In all, this voice impresses the soul so deeply that the Divine nature of it cannot be denied. With attention and practice, His voiceless voice can be heard and experienced more and more as an unmistakable reality.

The Gift of Being

To hear His voice, to be inspired by the Holy Spirit, to be stirred by the living presence of Jesus means to be caught up in the reality of His presence; in that moment one is cognizant of being inextricably united to Him and thus totally alive in the now. Without worry and agitation over the past and future, the depths of the soul quite freely yield to the utterances spoken by God. To hear His voice within, one need only turn inward to that still point of quietude and wait for His quiet whisperings.

Heaven is the realization of the gift of being. When the soul hears the voice of Jesus, it is at the same time acutely aware of the gift of being — of existing outside of time and space in His presence. The full realization of the gift of being at one moment fills the soul with heaven.

At a recent conference on healing and Christianity sponsored by the Christian Psychological Foundation, I witnessed a very saintly man heeding the voice of God. This conference was dedicated to providing inspiration and healing to all God's people. We brought in an internationally known healing evangelist widely respected in both Catholic and Protestant circles. As I watched him minister — pray with others for healing — I noticed that before doing so he would quiet himself and sense the leading of God's spirit. Once before his teaching he asked me to pray with him so that he might feel recollected and interiorly in tune with God. For five minutes we prayed together quietly in a small chapel area designated only for quiet reflection. At the end of this time, he looked at me and I looked at him, both of us aware of God's holiness within and without.

He gently walked to the podium and announced to over two hundred people that he felt we should move in a direction different from what we had anticipated. Rather than beginning the conference with teachings on physical healing, we would instead emphasize the healing of relationships. During our prayer time together, he heard the voiceless voice of God inspire him to teach on forgiveness and healing. As the result of following this inspiration, scores of individuals that evening attested to finding release from the bondage of toxic resentment that had plagued them for years.

The following day, the evangelist moved in a similar manner. After his final teaching, he closed his eyes and became very still. He sensed God's nudging and heard the voiceless voice prompting him to pray for physical healing. As he prayed, we witnessed the healing of physical pain, the straightening of bent limbs, the shrinking of tumors and relief from arthritis. Hearing and obeying the voiceless voice generated healing for body, mind, and spirit.

At the end of our conference, I felt healing coursing through me. I felt the wonder of being alive. Heaven saturated my soul. One man listening to the voiceless voice enabled all present to more attentively hear the voiceless voice in a personal way. In so doing, new dimensions of heaven opened up within each one of us. Speaking personally, I am now more clearly sensitized to discerning the voiceless voice. When I hear His voice within me, healing touches my soul.

Nothing so gratifies me as the joy of conversing with Jesus. When I hear His quiet inspirations, I am overwhelmed with gladness about being alive. What a gift He has given us — the gift of existing each moment and listening to the voiceless voice of Jesus.

In the words of one religious writer:

> The near presence of God's spirit may be experienced in its reality — indeed, only experienced. And the mark by which the spirit's existence and nearness are made irrefutably clear to those who have ever had the experience, is the utterly incomparable feeling of happiness which is connected with the nearness, and which is therefore not only a possible and altogether proper feeling for us to have here below, but is the best and most indispensable proof of God's reality.... No other proof is equally convincing, and therefore happiness is the point from which every efficacious new theology should start.

God's gift of being to each one of us is a gift from a whole and presumably happy creator to His created. Toxicity interferes with wholeness and happiness. It throws us off center, and we no longer feel at peace or content. A toxic person is an unhappy person.

Facing and working through toxic feelings enables one to reestablish the feeling of being centered in God, at peace with oneself and others. Of course, no one of us ever feels centered all of the time. Life, in many ways, is an ever unfolding opportunity to center ourselves more deeply in the Holy. We struggle. We are imperfect. But, none the less, our seeking allows us to grow in centeredness and wholeness, to grow out of toxicity and into health.

Feeling centered releases toxins from the human system. It is cleansing for the soul. A sense of being at peace and centered within is in itself a communication from His voiceless voice. The voice bids us peace, courage for the inner journey, and hope for continued release from toxic relationships.

His Voice — Each Moment of the Day

Our true gift is to be able to hear His voice each moment of the day. The magnificence of this gift lies in the fact that each of us retains the ever-present ability to tune in to God. We can listen to Him as the prophets of old listened to Him.

St. John of the Cross wrote:

> For God's spirit makes them know what must be known and ignore
> what must be ignored, remember what ought to be
> remembered...and forget what ought to be forgotten, and make
> them love what they ought to love, and keep them from loving
> what is not God.

This inner inspiration of the Holy Spirit brings to mind what needs to be brought to mind. Living in tune with God frees us of toxic concerns and issues, and even infuses supernatural love within the soul in such a manner that we are able to love and understand the unlovable. Each moment of each day He speaks, helping us to know, to remember, and to love.

The Spanish mystic continued: "At a particular time, a person will have to attend to a necessary business matter. He will not remember through any form, but without knowing how, the time and suitable way of attending to it will be impressed on his soul without fail."

In the most practical of matters, God provides guidance. Through the realization of the gift bestowed on each soul — the gift of hearing His voice — everyday guidance from God is a truth that can be relied upon. Without fail, the Holy Spirit creates thoughts, ideas, and motivations for accomplishing what is required in daily life. Such a gift God has provided — the gift of hearing Him each moment of the day.

Toxic relationships interfere with hearing God's voice. I have often listened to people complain, "All of a sudden I felt so out of touch with God. Literally, I felt cut off from Him, as though He no longer loved me." Everything seems so fine and, all of a sudden, some sort of toxic reaction takes place and makes a person feel estranged from God and his or her innermost self.

Albert, a regular churchgoer of the Eastern Catholic Rite, noted this concern. His particular parish focused so much on the outward form of religion that interior spirituality seemed all but lost. The people in the parish argued about this or that ritualistic observance. The priest would harangue the parishioners during his sermon with regard to minute details of church law. Slowly but surely, Albert felt sick at soul.

His dreams indicated that the people in his church were literally making him sick. He could no longer sense the presence of God when surrounded by these people. It was all so distracting and upsetting for him that he lost his steady centeredness in Jesus. Often, after Sunday

Mass, he became irritable, cranky, and depressed. He was suffering from a reaction to toxic relationships.

After many months of struggle, Albert decided to leave the parish. His Sunday malaise subsided. He found a smaller parish that preferred quiet and simple worship to extravagant ritualism. After Mass on Sundays, he now began to be quite content and spiritually rejuvenated.

To reestablish his own inner equanimity Albert needed to let go of unhealthy relationships. This required a severing of ties with his former parish. But, as he followed through with what he had to do, his soul returned to a state of health and, once again, he could hear God's voice in the depths of his soul.

Being — To Live and Breathe Jesus

Conversing with God throughout the day allows one to literally live and breathe Jesus. With each breath one takes, Jesus is drawn into the soul and toxins are released. Each moment one lives, Jesus lives in the soul. His voiceless voice communicates life and emotional and spiritual health. Living and breathing Jesus means that the soul of the human individual is gradually transformed into the image and likeness of Jesus.

Yves of Paris wrote:

This sublime knowledge tends less to the satisfaction of curiosity than to the ruling of life...for when I am aware of the first principle, I adore a Goodness without bounds; and in humility of feeling hope all from this cause which is formed all out of nothing.... when I contemplate a world that sprang from nothingness and which needs but an impulse to precipitate it into nothingness, I kiss the Hand which sustains it and gives it subsistence. All my love is His to Whom belongeth all.... How sweet are the thoughts that transport my spirit into that infinity which anticipated the world, accompanies it, and must succeed it!

So often we anguish and travail to hear the voice of God. All that is required is the simple realization that in Him we live, move, and have our being. True, not every moment of consciousness is one of conscious awareness of Him, but His grace always leads us onwards toward deeper dimensions of His reality and at times luxuriates the soul in a sensible awareness of the Divine. Ever onwards the soul is led, into greater depth of healing and wholeness.

Ultimately the cure of souls involves a heart-to-heart encounter with the Living Jesus. He alone is the ruling principle of life. He alone heals past wounds and emotional scars. Whether through medicine, intensive psychotherapy, or earnest prayer, Jesus who is a healing Jesus communicates a compassionate cure.

Whether consciously realized or not, without Jesus healing would not exist. The world and universe as we know it would deteriorate instantly into nothingness. In Him and through Him, healing pours forth into all manner of pain and dysfunction. His hand sustains all life. His gentle word, whether through the Scriptures or via the compassionate understanding of the doctor, cures the soul.

The awareness of Jesus — the heartfelt desire to live and breathe Jesus — helps to purify the soul from disabling toxins. Unhealthy relationships entangle one in a mess of confusion and discouragement. Problems and fears become the focus. Attention is given to tragedy and negativism. This is a sure sign of toxicity. Turning to Him, with the simple awareness of His presence, begins the process of cure.

A young patient of mine disclosed her lust for spiritual power. She greatly desired for others to look up to her. As one of the first females in her denomination to be ordained, she relished the acclaim and adulation. Power was all-important to her.

Although her demeanor appeared to be quite humble and spiritual, the drive for power possessed her. When she would not get her way, a dark mood would come over her. Negativism and depression took hold of her. She would then become more anxious, controlling, and impossible to live or work with. Toxicity of an interior nature threatened her emotional and spiritual well-being.

Finally, after much encouragement, she decided to enter into psychotherapy. Her symptoms of anxiety and discouragement had become so disabling that she had considered leaving the ministry. We soon realized that her push for power was, in itself, only a symptom. It betrayed the existence of a very bruised and bleeding self-esteem. On the inside she thought little of herself.

Quite subtly she had entered into a toxic relationship with power. It became the all-in-all for her. She sacrificed relationships with others and her own peace of mind for the sake of power. It overtook her with a vengeance. In a manner of speaking, she was possessed.

During the course of psychotherapy, her daily prayer life nurtured an awareness of the presence of Jesus that sustained us through the deep and turbulent waters that we were to pass. Her life of prayer settled her into her own depths and facilitated the cure of her soul. After almost three years of intensive work, a dream in which she saw herself lying prostrate before the crucified Jesus signaled that her release from possession by toxic power had taken place. A natural humility exuded from within her. Life and relationships, especially in her ministry, took on new meaning. Jesus, rather than an egocentric push for power, became the focus of her life.

Dark power, for her, was transformed into a healthy sense of self-esteem. His voice, felt during moments of quiet prayer throughout the day, provided the inspiration to continue along the inner journey. The inspiration sensed during prayer called her on into the depths of her soul. There where the tension of opposites is integrated and toxins are purged she knew firsthand the cure of her soul.

The Dark One

Do not put your trust in princes, in any child of Adam, who has no power to save. When his spirit goes forth he returns to the earth, on that very day all his plans come to nothing. How blessed is he who has Jacob's God to help him, his hope is in Yahweh, his God, Who made heaven and earth, the sea and all that is in them. He frustrates the wicked. Yahweh reigns forever, your God, Zion, from age to age. (Ps 1 46:3–10)

Not to trust any child of Adam means, psychologically, to relinquish destructive interpersonal and intrapsychic entanglements. All entanglements with inner forces, with other people, whether family or friends, are destructive. Real relationships are built upon understanding, freedom, and love. Entanglements, on the other hand, smack of hidden agendas, pressuring expectations, and possession.

When caught in an entangled relationship, individuals depend upon those they are entangled with for approval and acceptance. Typically, one of the most debilitating problems occurs between children and parents. Parents entangle children by attempting to possess them. In a highly unconscious manner parents project their own unlived ideals onto their children. Quite subconsciously, the child then feels impelled, and perhaps even driven, to live out the parents' unlived life. In such cases, the child feels highly dependent on his or her parents' approval. On the surface, parent and child seem to be close, but underneath this ostensibly loving relationship lurks the possession of the child by the parent and the hatred of the child toward the parent for this possession.

Darkness abounds in such an entangled relationship. The individual does not exist, since the human soul individuates via the cutting of interpersonal entanglements and the personal forging ahead in one's creative life despite all obstacles. Unconscious hatred, suppressed emotions, and unlived potentials characterize the darkness that plagues the downtrodden soul afflicted by entanglements. Interior oppression often made manifest in symptoms of anxiety and depression affects the imprisoned and blinded soul being led to and fro in the course of life by the need for approval and acceptance.

Often individuals do not consciously realize this interior slavery and darkness. Therefore, darkness is personified in the unconscious as "the dark one" or shadow — usually a dark figure of the same sex in one's dreams. A particular facet of unconsciousness, of oppression, of blindness, is dramatized by the dark one. While appearing in nightmarish forms, the dark one in reality is the voiceless voice of God.

The dark one is one who is oppressed, hungry, imprisoned, blinded, bowed down — one who is a stranger. The oppressed stranger within calls out for the healing touch of Jesus. Through the light of conscious awareness, God's grace touches the soul and gives justice to the oppressed, food to the hungry, freedom to the prisoner, sight to the blind, support for the bowed down, and protection for the stranger.

The love of Yahweh heals the upright soul — the one who diligently seeks His light and truth for all manner of darkness within. Darkness is not evil, nor is the dark one. Darkness and the dark one refer to all that still yearns to be brought into the healing light of Christ. In all things, in the light of Christ radiated into all manner of darkness, Jesus reigns supreme. Jesus reigns forever, your God, Zion, from age to age.

Dealing with the Dark One

Steve, a twenty-seven-year-old man, entered my office with a very forlorn and distraught look on his face. In his words, "I don't feel like living anymore. I just want to die. I can't find any reason to go on with my life."

During the first interview, I came to understand Steve's predicament. He had graduated from a very prestigious private high school in Chicago. He went on to complete four years of study at an Ivy League university, graduating in the top five percent of his class. Immediately he applied and was accepted to Harvard Law School. Without the slightest trace of difficulty, he breezed through his legal course work.

The day after his graduation from Harvard Law School, while his mother and father threw a big party, Steve retreated to his bedroom. He lay on his bed, stared at the ceiling, and truthfully admitted that he felt like dying. He knew that he could have a high paying job as a corporate attorney. He felt no desire for such prestige or professional advancement.

I recognized that he was truly at the end of his rope. He risked the possibility of taking his life. I took seriously his suicidal thoughts. He could do it if he didn't receive the help he needed. Together, we decided to try and understand his pain. In the many months to come, we discovered that indeed he was not his own man nor was he living his own life. Steve was living the life that his father never lived. His father, a wealthy Chicago businessman, had always dreamed of being a powerful attorney who would enter Chicago politics and enjoy the power and status therein. Since he never achieved this goal, he decided that his son would do it. Steve had been preordained by his father to become a powerful attorney and eventually a boss of Chicago politics.

In a desperate desire to please his father, Steve excelled at the best schools that money could provide. Finishing law school capped off his father's adulation and pride. In all of this, Steve felt depressed. He was not living the life that he needed to live.

His suicidal feelings reflected a deep truth. He needed to die to the life he was living — a life that he was living not for himself but for his father. Through psychotherapy he grew in emotional honesty and strength.

One day, he confidently entered our consultation room and remarked:

> I did it. I stood up to him. Once we finish our work in psychotherapy, I'll be leaving for New York to study music. Of course, my father's devastated. But, I'm exhilarated. For once, I had the courage to do what I really want to do.
>
> By the way, I had a dream last night. I was at some sort of family recreational center. I was jogging down the highway in front of the center. A very ominous-looking dark man sped down the highway in a recreational vehicle of some sort. I thought he was going to run me over. Rather than try to outrun his vehicle, so as to avoid getting hit, I stood right in the middle of the highway and faced this vehicle and this dark man. I guess he could have run me over, but in the dream I didn't think about it. I just had to face him.
>
> He not only did not run me over, but he pulled up alongside me and offered me a ride. I accepted his offer. No sooner had I sat down in the car than he began to drive off. He knew exactly where

he was going. He said he was going to take me home, to my own home. He went on to say, "You've come a long way."

When he said these words, I burst into tears and told him, "Yes, but I've lost my father, my father has died." He replied, "In a manner of speaking, yes, your father has died, but you have achieved a great deal." I did not understand the meaning of his words. Now that I'm talking, I realize that this family recreational center that I had left behind reminded me of my father — all the family entanglements and ties. In gaining my freedom, however, I felt the grief of losing my father.

I asked him what he meant in saying that I had achieved a great deal. The dark one replied, "In letting go of so much, you have also received so much." Once again I asked, "But what is it that I have achieved?" The dark one drove up to a home that was my home, my own home. As I stepped out of his car to move into my home, he stated with great gladness, "Eternal happiness is yours. It is what you have achieved." I awoke knowing that in leaving behind my own need to live for my father and my father's need for me to live for him, I had achieved my own identity and in this gained eternal happiness.

As can be seen in this dream, light shone through the darkness. The dark one symbolized many of his unconscious fears regarding the establishment of his own identity. Steve had long tried to outrun the need of his soul to grow up, to develop, to live his own life. With the grace he discovered in psychotherapy to confront his own toxic fears and through them to mature into a very unique and creative individual, he found the greatest treasure of all — his own God-given identity and with it, eternal happiness.

Healing a Man's Soul:
Moodiness or Holiness

A man's soul responds differently to the voice within than does a woman's soul. God seems to tailor-make his word for men and for women. He speaks to each individual in his or her own unique and distinct way, but He also communicates his inspiration differently depending upon the sex of the individual. This is due to the fact that a man's soul, its innate potentials and imbalances, is different than the soul of a woman.

A man, by nature, tends to be more cut and dry, less emotionally sensitive, more task-oriented as opposed to relationship-oriented, and more prone toward the outer world than the inner world. It is true that not all men fit into this sort of categorization; but, by and large, in our culture, men typically manifest a personality pattern very similar to that described. For this reason, men are especially in need of growth and development along the lines of increasing emotional and spiritual sensitivity. This includes the development of intuitive faculties, empathic understanding, and spiritual awakening. The drive toward the outer life needs the balance of greater interiority, of seeking the presence of Jesus within.

A man who flees from spiritual and emotional experiences soon becomes "possessed." Such possession takes the form of moodiness, irritability, and a generally cold feeling toward family and friends. Such a man has become possessed by his hidden-away and locked-up feelings. He can become quite intolerable to be around, to live with, and to understand. In point of fact, he has closed himself off to healing. His soul cries out for help, and, sooner or later, he must get the help he needs or suffer the risk of an emotional and spiritual breakdown, a toxic reaction to a psychic imbalance.

If the breakdown occurs, it usually takes place somewhere around mid-life. From thirty-five to forty-five years of age a man is prone toward suffering a spiritual crisis. It may take the form of him being convinced that he is in love with another woman, in need of a vocational change, or convinced that his life has been worthless. Suicide may present itself as the only recourse. In all of these cases, a man desperately needs to come to grips with his own soul — to a living encounter with the Risen Christ within him. He is indeed being called, called by God, to a radical change of life. But, the transformation is an interior matter, not a concern necessarily involving altering outer circumstances or relationships. If any changes in the outer world need to take place, it should be done only after a man has gone through intensive soul-searching with a trusted spiritual director or psychotherapist. The danger of a mid-life crisis lies in a man changing his outer world in hopes of bringing himself interior healing. Interior pain must be dealt with in an interior way. Turning within, coming to grips with unconscious feelings and attitudes, is the one and only hope for the man in crisis to find help and salvation.

The holy prophet Elijah knew the torment of possession by moodiness. After having severely dealt with over eight hundred false prophets, he heard that the Queen Jezebel was intent on killing him. This fearless man of God knew the power of the miraculous working through him.

Fire came down from heaven to earth via his prayers. Nothing seemed to stand in his way. Yet one woman, the woman Jezebel, threatened to demolish this hardy man of God.

The Old Testament records that upon hearing of Jezebel's threat to kill him within twenty-four hours, Elijah fled to the desert. He threw himself under a broom tree. Overwhelmed by depression and despair, he begged God to take his life. He felt no hope, no way out of his problem.

When a man has been possessed by a mood, a dark and gloomy sentiment, he perceives no way out of his dilemma. He can literally want to die. This, of course, does not mean that a solution does not exist, only that a man does not feel that there is a way out for him. The way through this crisis lies in turning to God, alone and with great intensity.

Many times I have witnessed wives attempt to talk their husbands out of their moods. But a man possessed by his mood cannot talk it out. He does not have a sense of what is happening to him. He needs to be encouraged to find a suitable spiritual director or psychotherapist, someone who will help him sort through his unresolved feelings about his life. In this manner, those who care can offer a man love via their support and encouragement without attempting to get him to talk about painful feelings that have literally swallowed him up. Under the broom tree he must go, to find God and hear the voiceless voice.

In actuality, a crisis in a man's life is the voiceless voice of God. Dark feelings in which he seems to drown are the nudging presence of the Savior. God beckons the man at this point in his life to come to terms with his soul and turn his life over in a new way to God. He must touch the hem of Jesus's garment. Through the fiery ordeal of his own life-crisis, he will come into a new relationship with God and those individuals that he loves.

God never fails to come through once we have endured what we must endure. Elijah, after wailing under the broom tree, was visited by an angel. This heavenly messenger touched him with spiritual refreshment and renewed vigor. Conversion, a life-changing experience with the Holy, always emerges out of a crisis that has been worked through.

Jesus bequeaths holiness out of moodiness. A forlorn and troubled man has the seeds of great holiness within him if he will but heed the voiceless voice. But, he must be willing to wail under the broom tree. Inevitably the cross precedes the glory. As with Jesus, so with every man: resurrection light dawns after the agony of crucifixion. We come to terms with deeply-held unconscious feelings and attitudes in the healing light of the Risen Jesus.

Julian of Norwich comments on darkness and light within the soul:

> Sometimes we experience such darkness that we lose all our energy. But our intent in life is to continue to live in God and faithfully trust that we will be shown compassion and grace. This is God's own working in us. Out of the goodness of God the eye of our understanding is opened by which we see, sometimes more and sometimes less, according to the ability we are given to receive.
>
> I saw the Soul so large as if it were an endless world and a joyful kingdom. And I understood that it is a beautiful City. In the midst of that city sits our Lord Jesus, God and one of us, a beautiful person of large stature clothed as befit his role as Bishop and King. And beautifully he sits, peacefully and restfully, in the Soul, his most familiar home and endless dwelling.

Healing a Woman's Soul

The voiceless voice speaks healing in the soul of a woman very differently than He does in the soul of a man. By nature, a woman is very intuitive, emotionally sensitive, and spiritually-minded. That is not to say that men do not have many of these qualities, but they are more pronounced in women of our time and culture. God realizes this and speaks according to the potential of a woman to hear His voice.

I believe that there are at least four characteristics of a healthy and holy woman. A woman who is in touch with her soul experiences herself and life in certain ways. Such a woman is humble, holy, merciful, and loving.

A Humble Woman

> My soul proclaims the greatness of the Lord and my spirit rejoices in God my Savior. (Lk 1:46)

From heartfelt emotion, a woman's soul is God-focused. Very naturally her soul proclaims the majesty of Yahweh. God, in all of His splendor made manifest in day-to-day events, fills her every waking moment. She is quite definitely not always consciously aware of the Gift but her unconscious mind constantly abides in Him. The Holy of Holies resides within her.

A man frequently finds himself in need of some sort of external challenge or activity to prove himself, to touch the Holy. As a matter of psychological development, each man lives his life in such a way as to master that which he is called to do in the world. Frequently, his search for God is taken up by having to experience many external crises that finally bring him to his knees before a Savior who loves him. Saul of Tarsus blazed furiously down the Damascus road, doing what he thought he needed to do. God literally knocked him off his horse and turned his heart toward Him. Elijah, the great prophet of old, fled from Queen Jezebel and hid himself under the broom tree. Out of his experience of dark torment came the voiceless voice of Yahweh that healed his soul.

Mary, the mother of Jesus, never needed such an external drama to turn her heart humbly and purely to her savior. We can imagine that the day the angel visited her was like any other day in her life. She proceeded about her daily activities, one of which was a regular time of prayer. On this particular day, which was like any other day in her life, an angel visited her. Every woman carries the Holy within her. She need not seek outside herself for Him. Her way is a profoundly inner way.

When a woman moves against her interiority, she loses touch with her soul. She soon becomes prone toward being arrogant and power-ridden. She often feels harried by a multitude of activities and yet feels incredibly lacking in interior fulfillment. When a woman looks outside of herself for life, nourishment, and sustenance she loses contact with Jesus Who lives within her. She becomes toxic.

A woman who places priority on her interior life maintains a constancy of focus on God and therein walks in humility. By and large, she is able to sense an equanimity and tranquility in her life. Outer ministry and work proceed from the wholeness of life in her soul. God, not outer achievements and accomplishments, gently guides her ever onwards.

The Holy Woman

> ...because He has looked upon the humiliation of His servant. Yes, from now onwards all generations will call me blessed, for the Almighty has done great things for me. Holy is His name, and His faithful love extends age after age to those who fear him. (Lk 1:48–49)

God's holiness settles into the heart of a woman who diligently seeks Him. Holiness is the experience of God that transforms the soul into His image and likeness, increasingly free of spiritual toxins. To experience God means to be touched, healed, and made whole.

Without holiness, a woman feels energized by ego-centered anxieties. Such a woman seems quite filled up with herself. In every conversation she needs to have the last word. In her mind, her own personal opinions and ideas definitely are more important than those of others. She carries herself with a haughtiness and arrogance that offends others, but she is almost never confronted by others due to her inability to listen, to reflect on herself and to understand the meaning of her actions.

Sister Mary Theresa cornered me after I had finished an afternoon lecture to a group of retreatants. She asked sincerely:

> For so long I have faithfully prayed a holy hour every day. I never felt God's presence, His holiness before. Just lately, after working through a lot of painful memories in my own psychotherapy, I am sensing His love for me. Why am I sensing His love for me now? Did all those years of previous prayer go to waste?

I saw the look of concern in her eyes. For so many years she prayed in a disciplined way, yet never really encountered the Holy. Now, the greatness of God had dawned upon her. She felt Him through and through. She spoke so tenderly and genuinely. What did all of those years of prayer mean for her?

I reflected carefully, then felt an inspiration to answer in the following way: "Sister, your years of prayer prepared you for what you are now savoring. Your years of prayer stored up grace upon grace in your soul. From now on, through eternity, you will witness the unfolding majesty of God's grace in your heart."

Through many tears she replied:

> I do feel that this is true. You know, I used to put other people off. They said I walked with my nose held in the air, like I was arrogant and above them. I really did not feel that way on the inside. In fact, I really was quite intimidated by people. I played the role of being above it all because I really felt so defeated on the inside. As I come into knowing God on a heart-to-heart basis, really knowing Him, it seems as though people like me more. In fact, I like people more. The better God and I get along, the better people and I get along. His grace, His Holy Grace, is being unwrapped within me moment by moment and day by day.

A holy woman gradually but surely knows the God experience. Rather than ego-centered, arrogant living, she carries herself with a holiness that causes her to be seen as approachable. Intuitively, others know that she will understand and have compassion for their pain. A holy woman is a woman who has heard His voiceless voice.

A Merciful Woman

Mercy follows holiness. A merciful woman knows God's compassion. So easily a woman extends herself to others. So easily she gives and gives and gives. Without intending to do so, a woman can overextend herself. For the female psyche, saying "yes" is second nature. The ability to say "no," to set limits and abide by them, requires much growth and self-understanding. In such a way, a woman learns to become merciful toward herself. Instead of running herself ragged, she now maintains an interior composure and allegiance to what she can and cannot do.

The psalmist maintains, "his faithful love extends age after age to those who fear him" (Lk 1:50). His faithful love, His mercy, is a heartfelt oneness with the Divine. God's mercy enables the human soul to exercise merciful compassion with regard to its own abilities and limitations. Thus, overextending oneself is never in line with the will of God. He is merciful to us and beckons us to be merciful to ourselves.

Martha, a middle-aged Catholic housewife, had for so long felt bedraggled and at wit's end. She was the busy mother of five children. Along with this, she was president of the Women's Guild in her parish, as well as serving as den mother and homeroom mother. She felt that this incessant activity was legitimate for her personally since it helped so many people. She was able to offer support and encouragement to the women of the parish, the cub scouts, the parish school, and anyone else who needed her help. The only problem was that she suffered from chronic irritability, tension, and unrelenting headaches.

Finally, she had the following dream:

A man was calling to me from the third story of a building that was crumbling. I was standing on the sidewalk below and looking up at him. He called out, "How long do I have to stay working in this building? Won't you let me come down now? If I don't stop working soon, this whole building's going to fall down on top of me."

This dream reflected the critical nature of her situation. Very often in women's dreams, a man symbolizes the state of her soul. In this case, the man represented the way her soul felt overextended, over-worked, and ready to collapse. She needed to be more merciful with herself. As she heeded the voiceless voice of God coming in and through this dream, her symptoms decreased.

She soon relinquished many of her parish activities. With more leisure time on her hands, she was able to feel more relaxed and at ease. Well-being and contentment replaced anxiety and headaches. Merciful living is healthy living.

Woman — Preachy and Pushy or Loving

A distressed woman, suffering from emotional toxins, often can come across quite preachy and pushy. She seems to have an opinion about everything under the sun. She preaches about the way things are, should be, and will be if she has anything to do about it. Everything in life is forced and pushed together. Manipulation and forcefulness characterize a woman who is out of touch with her soul.

Contrary to this, a woman whose heart has been made alive with the experience of love radiates a quiet strength. She is not a doormat to be walked over; but neither is she a blasting trumpet sounding off on every available occasion. She knows who she is and who she is not. Because of this, she does not waste energy trying to do a multitude of diverse and disconnected tasks. She is focused and therefore she is loving.

Mary completes the Magnificat with great exultation and worship: "He has come to the help of Israel his servant, mindful of his faithful love — according to the promise He made to our ancestors — of His mercy to Abraham and to his descendants forever" (Lk 1:54–55).

Mary's receptive love changed the course of salvation history. Generation after generation would feel the bounty of God's blessing. Her loving, quiet, and strong soul received Jesus and helped to create the experience of life-transforming love for all generations to come.

When a woman undergoes a transformation of love in her own heart, her children and her children's children will be profoundly influenced. Children learn more from who a woman is than from what she teaches. The love in her soul is absorbed by her children. Her loving presence is internalized, quite unconsciously, by them. Her descendants will be people alive with the love of God, just as her being was alive with the love of God.

Paraphrasing a spiritual parable, a young mother wonderfully described how hearing the voiceless voice awakened her heart to love and to life:

I used to fail to understand why saints — and lovers —
behaved the way they did. So I was waiting for my heart to come
alive.

I used to be stone deaf. I would see people stand up and go
through all kinds of gyrations. They called it dancing.

It looked absurd to me — until one day I heard the music!

And now my heart is alive!

The Revealer of Mystery

And now to Him who can make you strong in accordance with the
gospel that I preach and the proclamation of Jesus Christ, in
accordance with that mystery which for endless ages was kept
secret but now [as the prophets wrote] is revealed, as the eternal
God commanded, to be made known to all the nations, so that they
obey in faith; to Him, the only wise God, give glory through Jesus
Christ forever and ever. (Rom 16:25–27)

Jesus was the mystery which was kept secret, but is now revealed to all
those who earnestly seek truth. The voiceless voice communicates itself
via mystery. Christ Jesus is the mystery par excellence. Living deeply in
Jesus means to understand ever more profoundly the mystery of His
presence dwelling within.

Living within the ever-unfolding mystery of Christ strengthens the
soul. Mystery, the ever-unfolding depths of the unconscious, nourishes
and heals the soul. Without mystery, one's life is left sterile, bland, and
weak. The experience and knowledge of mystery awakens dormant faculties, potentials, and encounters with the God of all creation.

Through images and symbols of the Holy, the mystery of Christ
Jesus becomes manifest. Images and symbols convey a numinous quality that transforms the soul without words ever being spoken. Symbols
of the Holy radiate the living presence of Jesus in an awesome manner
that bypasses both logic and, at times, intellectual comprehension.
Through images and symbols of the Holy, the Divine Mystery is
revealed. And therein, toxins are worked out of one's soul and one's relationships.

The Healer

The symbol of the healer, frequently occurring in dreams, reflects one of
the most powerful expressions of the Holy — God's voiceless voice.
The holy person or group of holy people appear in a night vision to the

soul in need of a cure. Through the tumbles and scrapes of life, internal bleeding and damage can be sustained. The voice of Jesus, expressing itself through the healing symbol, brings refreshment and wholeness within.

The healer comes in both obvious and paradoxical forms. The more in touch one is with the interior life, the more the symbol is clear and concise. The more cut off we are from our feelings, the more roundabout and even frightening is the symbol. Thus, not all apparently terrifying images in dreams are representing demonic or disintegrating forces; they may, in fact, be the voiceless voice of God.

The most terrifying of encounters in dreams can bespeak enormous healing potential. Feelings that have been long repressed and viewed as evil, take evil form in the dream world. They appear grotesque and distorted, but offer soothing and healing if faced and integrated. As you face what you fear, as interior darkness is integrated, a healing balm pours forth.

A young man came to a surprising awareness:

> I had been afraid that the devil was trying to get me in my dreams. For many nights I dreamed of a contorted demon-like figure who was trying to touch me. Out from the pores of his hands issued a jelly-like substance. In the dream I thought it was gross; but, now that I think about it, it reminds me of balm. When I was in athletics, we used to rub a substance very much like the one I saw in my dream on sore muscles and on any scrapes or bruises that were inflicted during the game. So, now I see. This little creature actually ministers healing to me if I will let him touch me.
>
> His contortions made him look angry. I think I'm contorted with anger on the inside. I have been so afraid of my anger that I have pushed it away. I thought it wasn't Christian to be angry. Now, I think I have a lot to learn about my anger, and, as I do, a lot of my inner hurts and bleeding will be healed.

To this young man, the symbol of healing — the healer — emerged in a quite frightful way. God wants to get our attention no matter what He has to do to get it. The most terrifying of images that arise out of the unconscious may be harbingers of well-being if we have eyes to see and ears to hear. The intensity of God's numinous light shining within the soul may, in fact, feel quite terrifying before we experience its healing effect.

At other times, the healer comes forth in a more straightforward manner. Herman, a middle-aged man who was recently coming to terms with his own history of having been sexually abused, noted the following dream:

> In my dream, I saw Dr. DeBlassie helping me to take off layer upon layer of material that was covering my body. I was all covered up. As we gently rolled away the last layer of this tissue-fine material, four angelic women arose from inside of me. They looked like angels, shining brightly with an unearthly light surrounding them. They softly but definitely uttered, "We bring you healing from the kingdom."

I remember when Herman told me about this dream. He burst into a flood of tears. For many months we had struggled to realize the depth of his pain regarding his sexual abuse. He had not been able to cry. Psychotherapy felt like we were journeying through a desert: it was tough and arid work.

After sharing this dream, he changed. His tears brought depth of feeling. Terror, anger, grief, vindictiveness, and finally, settledness surged out of him. Healing from psychic toxins came after many months of preparatory work via the emergence of a symbol of the healer — four angels speaking the words of His voiceless voice.

The Revealer

In the Old Testament, the prophet Daniel refers to Yahweh as the Revealer of Mysteries. In interpreting the dream of Nebuchadnezzar, Daniel remarks:

> Your Majesty, on your bed your thoughts turn to what would happen in the future, and the Revealer of Mysteries disclosed to you what is to take place. This mystery has been revealed to me, not that I am wiser than anyone else, but for this sole purpose: That the king should learn what it means, and that you should understand your inmost thoughts. (Dn 2:29–30)

The voiceless voice reveals the inmost thoughts of the heart. That which either escapes consciousness or is denied as personal truth surfaces as one diligently seeks God. Coming to know one's inmost thoughts coincides with the increasing knowledge of Yahweh.

Holy symbols and images arising from the depths of the soul reveal these innermost mysteries. Through understanding the truths that the holy symbol imparts, one's life can be lived more harmoniously, productively, and toxin-free. Without such guidance, we can often live at cross purposes with ourselves and with God. We attempt to do what is truthful and right in our life only to find out that we secretly harbor hidden agendas that inevitably create chaos within and without. Rather than experiencing the pain of unresolved interior darkness, it is best to unwrap such a mystery and find the gift within it. That is to say, the discovery of mystery means understanding the meaning of personal suffering and the inherent growth and blessing it provides. In a sense, then, mystery is purposeful. It creates newness and life, an ever-expanding wonder and awe with one's self, other people, and life in general. Yahweh breathes freshness and vitality into the soul that explores and understands mystery.

Such a perspective entails the realization that God cannot and will not be boxed in or contained by static ideas. My wife, Kathy, appreciates the wisdom of a noted author who asserts, "My religion is subject to change without notice." Jesus is the same yesterday, today, and forever. But, our human understanding of Him, hopefully, deepens with each passing moment. Therefore, as our spirituality changes, so do many of our ideas and expressions.

The Revealer visits the soul as "a voice of one that cries in the desert: Prepare a way for the Lord. Make His paths straight!" (Jn 1:23). Unfolding mysteries reestablish balance in the human personality. In areas that one felt conflict, pride, or dormancy, the Revealer straightens the path for the influx of grace. Jesus pours forth wholeness, balance, and new creativity as inner secrets are unlocked.

Frank, a very intuitive and insightful twenty-eight-year-old man, asked me if smoking marijuana was evil. Surprised at the extreme nature of his question, I asked why it concerned him. He replied that since his spiritual conversion, he had let go of a great many past excesses, notably in regard to his sexual behavior and imbibing of alcohol. But, he, at times, greatly enjoyed smoking marijuana.

Five or six times a year, he took great delight in "toking up." I had to admit that Frank seemed quite sincere in doubting whether smoking marijuana was actually detrimental to him physically, spiritually, and emotionally. On one level, he did not feel any danger in this pastime. On the other hand, something deep inside him stirred and urged him on to take a closer look at his habit.

Frank finally reported the following dream:

> I was in a room, a very dark room, all by myself. I had a funny feel-
> ing in this room. Out of nowhere, two red eyes darted out at me.
> They chased me all over the room. I was haunted by them. I was
> terrified and panic-stricken by their evil and devilish gaze.

Frank and I together understood the meaning of this dream. This
dark room was the very room in which he frequently smoked marijuana.
He needed to see something about this seemingly innocent activity.
God's grace mandated that he enter into a full understanding of his secret
and hidden behavior. "Getting stoned" dulled his feelings and his perception of God's presence. Smoking pot numbed his soul. This was an evil
of inescapable reality.

The dream so jarred Frank that he immediately abandoned the smoking of marijuana. In his words:

> I'd rather tune in than numb out. Life feels wonderful when I tune in
> to God. After getting stoned, I always pay the price of sluggish-
> ness and feeling down. I've seen what I needed to see about
> marijuana. It's time for me to give it up. Now that the secret is out
> in the open, I'm free to be tuned in rather than numbed out.

The Ever-Unfolding Mystery

The voiceless voice of Yahweh beckons one forth to the potent realization that He is the Ever-Unfolding Mystery. Without such knowledge,
humans regress to a toxic identification of one sort or another. That is to
say, we identify with and cling to externals that cause us to believe that
we have finally, completely, and thoroughly understood God and the
nature of all things. Usually, this comes in the form of various "isms."

Movements, such as those found in both church and professional
circles, hold out the illusion of finally having "made it." One may not
consciously admit to such truth; it may be cloaked with sayings such as,
"We're all on the way together," "No one of us has it made," or "We're
no better than anyone else." In reality, we often harbor secret notions
that we have, in fact, found a superior way of approaching God. Consciously or unconsciously, this precipitates a condescending manner in
dealing with others. It also expels us from the true realm of mystery.

The *mysterium tremendum* imposes a watchfulness, a silence, and a
reverential awe to all initiates. The experiences of the ever-unfolding
mystery humbles the soul and causes one to live life fully with other

people without pretense and without arrogance. Such a person solidly grasps his or her own identity and, therefore, rests secure in the arms of life. The only certainty is the truth that the ever-unfolding mystery infuses one's personal life with both constant change and increasing settledness.

When Yahweh's voiceless voice communicates the reality of His ever-unfolding mystery, at least three healing inspirations unfold: *live deeply, love God, and let go.*

Live Deeply

One evening after completing a lecture on Christian depth psychology, an older gentleman feverishly approached me at the podium. He anxiously demanded, "I just want you to understand what I'm going through. I've had it with life. Nothing is going my way." I finally interrupted him and said, "I believe I understand you, but not in the way that you had hoped. Your life is not all that bad. You are just afraid to change, to flow with the new developments in your life. You want to hide behind self-pity and depression. Life is on your side. Flow with it, live deeper, and you will be happy."

Stunned, he admitted that after having lived almost sixty years of life in a very extroverted manner, he now felt God calling him to a quieter and more contemplative way. In his mind, he interpreted this as defeat — letting go of everything that was really important in life.

His whirlwind of business activities, superficial socializing, and indulgences of one kind or another were slowing down. He despaired of losing a foothold on life in the way that he knew it. He also sensed that this mysterious unfolding and calling to a quieter and more contemplative, more prayerful life was indeed a calling from God.

As we left that evening, he felt a clearer understanding and a definite challenge ahead of him. He could either grow more anxious, more neurotic, more toxic, or choose to give in to the ever-unfolding mystery that now called him to self-reflection and interior quietude. I hope, for his sake, that he decided to follow the inner way and heed the voiceless voice. The exquisite joy and deep riches that flow from living life deeply are supremely worth the sacrifice of leaving all to follow Him.

Love God

The unfolding mystery of Jesus Christ experienced in the depths of the soul is always accompanied by a fervent love of God. Thus, the Revealer of Mystery enters into a relationship of love with the believer. In this relationship, one must not identify with the Mystery or even unconsciously relate to it as though it were a possession or an entitlement. Rather, the love of God keeps one Christ-centered and involved in the continual process of dying to egocentricities, and experiencing an ongoing cure from inward toxins.

In this manner, we keep an ever-constant awareness of our inability to truly love in return for the love received from God. Only in and through His grace can we love. In fact, as one grows increasingly conscious of the Mystery, interior illnesses and shortcomings become evermore apparent. This serves to maintain a humility of heart in light of the ever-flowing revelation of the Mystery.

St John of the Cross wonderfully expressed this exquisite love of God:

> O living flame of love
> That tenderly wounds my soul
> In its deepest center! Since
> Now You are not oppressive,
> Now Consummate! If it be your will:
> Tear through the veil of this sweet encounter!
>
> O sweet cautery,
> O delightful wound!
> O gentle hand! O delicate touch
> That tastes of eternal life
> And pays every debt!
> In killing You changed death to life.
>
> O lamps of fire!
> In whose splendors
> The deep caverns of feeling
> Once obscure and blind,
> Now give forth so rarely, so exquisitely,
> Both warmth and light to their Beloved.
>
> How gently and lovingly
> You wake in my heart,
> Where in secret You dwell alone;
> And in Your sweet breathing,
> Filled with good and glory,
> How tenderly You swell my heart with love.

Let Go

Following Jesus purposefully leads us to greater and greater relinquishment of egocentric concerns. That is to say, the ability to let go comes as a grace that enhances personal growth and well-being. Holding onto old attitudes disrupts that developmental process. Relinquishment, on the other hand, encourages steadfast movement toward the likeness of the Risen Jesus.

The failure to let go at appropriate times in one's life results in quackery. By "quackery" I mean false ways of relating to others that may have been valid and appropriate at one point in one's life but are no longer viable. To press ahead with untruths induces immaturity and a sense of being a lost soul. Gradually, such an individual degenerates into a person experiencing burnout and isolation.

In the healing professions, quackery abounds whenever the soul is abandoned. A physician, for example, may be a highly skilled technician, but be greatly lacking in human empathy. Thus, the essential ingredient of all healing is not present. This causes the physician to approach patients in a rather stilted and forced manner that may actually inhibit the process of healing. On the contrary, an empathic and technically skilled physician brings authentic healing to his or her patients. In this case, the physician is a healer — in the truest sense of the word.

When I supervised graduate students in clinical psychology at Northwestern University School of Medicine, I noticed an interesting trend. Frequently, they began their clinical years very interested in techniques that avoided the unconscious, such as behavior modification, cognitive therapy, or other intrusive and manipulative measures. After approximately three or four years of treating patients with these directive approaches, they became disillusioned. A quality of depth and understanding of the soul had been severely lacking. This usually precipitated a crisis, both professionally and personally, for the psychological intern.

Thankfully, this crisis led many of them into personal psychotherapy. There they learned to understand themselves in a more in-depth manner. They experienced the depth and rightness of the unconscious firsthand. This powerful healing encounter ushered them into a new way of relating to their patients.

One student in particular commented, "I can no longer treat my patients with behavior modification or cognitive techniques. Healing is more than the application of the technique. The healing of the soul requires empathy and feeling. To do less than this for me would be quackery."

Healers need to let go of old and unempathic ways of relating to others. As human understanding occurs, growth occurs. Attempting to facilitate the process of letting go of unfeeling ways of relating to others is never easy. At times, one is not even aware that he or she has been cold or lacking in heart. Once the awareness surfaces, growth and consciousness have commenced. To turn back or to close one's eyes creates a deliberate falseness in relating — creates quackery, and a toxic "healer."

It should be noted that a most important role for parents is that of healer. When harshness and unreasonable demands take the place of gentle listening and understanding, falsity abounds. Children abhor such tyranny. The results inevitably are childhood depression, teenage rebellion, chronic family conflict, and perhaps even hospitalization. Children need authentic parents, not "quacky" parents.

Parents must let go of insensitivity and demanding authoritarianism, and grow into a firm empathy toward their children: then health and well-being can settle into family relationships. Parents may opt to hold on to the old way since the new way requires patience, self-examination, and a constant humility that underscores the fact that no one of us knows it all. With this gentleness, children actually help the parents to become better parents. Children assist the parents in understanding what is fair, what is firm as opposed to harsh, and what real is all about. Real parents never pretend to be perfect; only "quacky," toxic parents insist on their own perfection. Real parents know that just as their children are imperfect, so are they themselves imperfect. This calls for a very human empathy and sensitivity, all the while remaining truer to a firm, rather than a harsh, discipline of child rearing.

CONCLUSION
Toxicity and the Voiceless Voice

Both holiness and toxicity are felt experiences. Toxicity creates an interior writhing and disharmony. Holiness creates inner harmony and growth. The voiceless voice of Jesus speaking within the soul illuminates toxicity and imbues the soul with increasing holiness.

Holiness, in essence, is the living experience of God in the soul. The voiceless voice, whether felt through inner inspiration, the images and symbols in dreams, or through a personal revelation of mystery, moves one closer to holiness, to wholeness. Toxicity in life is inevitable. At some time or another, we, perhaps unconsciously and inadvertently, expose ourselves to unhealthy relationships or situations. We end up leaving such people or predicaments feeling out of sorts and filled with an inner dis-ease. We leave feeling infected with emotional and spiritual toxins. At such times, our relationship with God can see us through. Uniting ourselves with Him via prayer, spiritual direction, and/or psychotherapy helps us to hear His voiceless voice that resounds with healing for our infected soul.

The healing effect of union with God is powerfully related in the following widely told story:

> There was a terrible drought in that part of China where a young scholar was living. After all the ways to bring rain that the people knew had been tried, they decided to send for a rainmaker. This interested the young scholar very much, and he was careful to be there when the rainmaker arrived. The man came in a covered cart, a small wizened old man who sniffed the air with evident distaste as he got out of the cart, and asked to be left alone in a small cottage outside the village; even his meals were to be laid down outside the door.
>
> Nothing was heard from him for three days, then, it not only rained, but there was also a big downfall of snow, unknown at that time of the year. Very much impressed, the young scholar sought the rainmaker out and asked him how it was that he could make rain, and even snow. The rainmaker replied, "I have not made the snow; I am not responsible for it." The young scholar insisted there was a terrible drought until he came, and then after three days, they even had quantities of snow. The old man answered, "Oh, I can explain that. You see, I come from a place where the people are in order; they are in harmony with God; so the weather is also in order. But, directly I got here, I saw the people were out of order and they also infected me. So, I remained alone until I was once more deeply in harmony with God. And then, of course, it rained and snowed."

Three

God's Will for Your Life

God's will makes itself known via moment-to-moment graces. Human need and Divine Providence meet throughout life. Since the soul is made for God and God for the soul, Jesus can be counted on to provide for human need, growth, and development. At each step along life's way, He is there with fresh grace for new problems and new developments.

Thus, God always wills human growth. In all sectors of life, whether in the church, in science, or in finance and industry, God's grace is plentifully available. Releasing hidden potentials glorifies God. In this manner, men and women serve each other, always benefiting the common good, and therein serve God. Creativity and soundness of enterprise are always the hallmark of God's will.

The discerning of Divine Providence requires only an openness of heart so as to see the reality of the grace of the moment. Without such openness, we plod and stumble along through life like blind oxen. Having eyes to see and ears to hear His movement enables harmonious and relational living. In every moment of every day, His will unfolds and all that is asked of us is a humble cooperation with the grace of the moment.

Going against the grain of life, going against God's will, imposes toxicity onto life. Life is made to be challenging, yet harmonious. A toxic life manifests itself as chaotic and conflict-ridden. Nothing seems to go right. A life out of touch with God's will becomes cumbersome, despairing — it becomes toxic. God's moment-to-moment grace comes in unexpected realizations and insights. What one has considered to be good may suddenly be seen as contrary to God's will. In such a case a new direction in life emerges. A person is called to leave behind toxic lifestyles and attitudes, and gradually move into healthful living.

Thus, the cure of souls frequently witnesses significant life changes. Relationships change. Sometimes one's work and professional life change. One's religious life may even drastically change.

A middle-aged man felt sure that his road to salvation lay in continuing steadfastly in his church work. For so many years he had volunteered innumerable hours to the work of his parish. Unfortunately, this often left him without the expected spiritual nourishment and growth. In fact, his over-involvement in church work caused him to feel depleted and weary.

The anxiety with regard to church involvement left him questioning what he had earlier taken for granted. Perhaps he was too involved in outer parish life, to the neglect of his inner life. The lack of peace in his life suggested that this was so. Without realizing it, he had been out of step with God's will for his life and therefore leading a toxic life.

In a dream he found himself completely filled and surrounded by the presence of God right in the middle of a golf course. Somewhat stunned, he asked me:

> What can this mean? I thought God was only to be found in church. But, I have to admit that I sometimes sense more peace and harmony on the golf course than I do in my many church activities. I think I may need to ease up on how much I am doing and take more time for enjoyment. For me, the enjoyment of life, I have to admit, draws me nearer to God.

As this man slowly changed his life style, he found himself to be at peace and happy. He no longer worked quite so hard in his parish. He took more time for quiet and prayer. He took more time for the enjoyment of life in things that he enjoyed such as classical concerts, racquet ball, and golf. He moved away from a toxic life and moved closer to God as he learned of God's will for his life.

A Hidden Order

A hidden order flows through life. For one who earnestly seeks Him, all things work together for the good. That is to say, there are no accidents or coincidences — only God incidents. He orders all the details of life so as to accord with His specific and general will.

He is a God of order. What may seem to be chaotic problems and disjointed events always maintain a hidden order. It often takes time and distance to discern this definite meaning, but it will emerge with patience and steadfastness. During the tumult of crisis, meaning may be hard to find. After the storm of life passes, however, one usually recognizes God's plan and order. A watchful patience always discloses Divine intention.

Every Wednesday evening I consult with eight to twelve cardiac patients. Inevitably, the majority of them comment on the frantic pace

of their life prior to their heart attack. All the richness and zest of life
was depleted through their busy and anxious living.

After a heart attack, priorities often shift. Life is frequently lived in
a slower, more deliberate manner. One man chuckled as he confided:

> I used to feel that I was indispensable. My wife pointed out that the
> cemetery is filled with indispensable people. I am taking time now
> to enjoy my life. I work less and enjoy more. It actually took this
> crisis for God to change my life.
>
> Without being too presumptuous, I hope, I can actually admit
> that I feel a little wiser. The things that used to bother me don't
> bother me nearly as much. God is always at work in my life help-
> ing me to enjoy life and love Him and others more. He has been
> trying to get through to me my whole life long. The only differ-
> ence now is that I can hear Him. I was too busy to hear Him before.
> Life is sure a whole lot better for me now that I live in God and can
> actually feel His grace. I am in His will now.

St. Paul writes of the Divine will, "That is why, ever since the day
He told us, we have never failed to remember you in our prayers and ask
that through perfect wisdom and spiritual understanding, you should
reach the fullest knowledge of his will" (Col 1:9). Scripturally, wisdom
and understanding refer to two different ways of knowing God's will.
Wisdom suggests a knowledge of His general will. Jesus desires for
humankind to live centered in Him. In general, this is His will for
humanity.

Spiritual understanding focuses on the knowledge of God's will
regarding the specifics, the details, of everyday life. God's interest is not
only in the big picture, but also in the daily occurrences in your life. To
see His will unfolding in daily occurrences is to cultivate spiritual understanding.

Intuitively knowing the will of Jesus, both in general and in the
details of life, means that one recognizes that an ordered universe
surrounds us and fills us. An underlying meaning flows out of all of
life's experiences. Needless to say, this evokes feelings of reverence and
awe in the living of everyday life.

God Incidences

St. Paul continues in his letter to the Colossians, "...and so be able to
lead a life worthy of the Lord, a life acceptable to Him in all its aspects,
bearing fruit in every kind of good work and growing in knowledge of
God" (Col 1:10). To lead a life worthy of the Lord calls for discernment,

becoming aware of His presence in every incident in life. For the believer, coincidences do not exist. Related happenings do not occur by accident. Rather the believer intuitively feels the interrelationship and unity of all life. God incidences, not coincidences, dynamically harmonize the universe.

Recent medical research confirms that healthy people maintain a joyful and vital attitude toward life. Far more than controlling risk factors such as smoking, cholesterol levels, blood pressure, and genetic background, the secret of health lies in the ability to flow with life joyfully. Biblically, this means to live a life worthy of the Lord.

Typically, individuals who are spiritually, emotionally, and physically healthy expect the best out of life. They very intuitively and naturally expect their lives to work out well. They anticipate that others appreciate and like them. Their world is a world of order and enjoyment.

Interestingly enough, healthy people seem to suffer their fair share of difficulties in the form of family problems, financial setbacks, and other such problems. Despite this fact, they continually refocus on the possibility of a brighter future. This unrelenting optimism opens the mind to God's grace — to God incidences — to the reestablishment of prosperity and order in their lives.

One noted medical researcher commented on President Reagan's undying optimism. When questioned about his colon cancer, he responded, "I didn't have cancer. I had something inside me that had cancer inside it, and it was removed." A healthy person sees himself or herself as thoroughly healthy, and sees dis-ease of body or spirit as an intruder that must be removed. Health is expected and health is received.

Life flows together for us as we flow with life. Jesus, who is Life, comes through most easily for us as we perceive ourselves as part of life. Order, harmony, and the providential coming together of events characterize what life is meant to be for us. Nothing short of health, well-being, and freedom from toxicity are meant for your life. God arranges incidents, inspires people, and bestows His grace in every conceivable manner in order to usher in His will for your life.

In summing up the characteristics of the religious life, William James notes the following:

1. That the visible world is part of a more spiritual universe from which it draws its chief significance;
2. That union or harmonious relation with that higher universe is our true end;

3. That prayer or inner communion with the spirit thereof — be that spirit "God" or "law" — is a process wherein work is
really done, and spiritual energy flows in and produces effects,
either psychological or material, within the phenomenal world.

Anything less than these phenomena described by James places one
potentially in a toxic "space." To see everything as related to a spiritual
universe harmonizes and wonderfully orders life. Without such an understanding, the soul is prone toward a type of egocentricity that breeds
anxiety and tension. In this context, a toxic life is a life that refuses to
acknowledge the hidden order — a hidden spiritual order — of which the
visible world is only a part.

To continue attending to this deep and inner spiritual world enables
the soul to live in union and harmony with life. In fact, as the years go
on, life has the potential to become more gentle and peaceful. Toxic
people know nothing of this experience. Life, to them, becomes a tortu-
ous movement from one crisis to another, each of which leaves them
more downcast and despairing than before. The soul attuned to the hidden
spiritual order knows his or her whole share of crises but, from each one,
greater growth and settledness in life are realized.

When primary importance is given to inner communion with the
spirit, practical life changes occur. In the words of James, "spiritual
energy flows in and produces effects, either psychological or material,
within the phenomenal world." For this reason, the toxic-ridden soul
knows only a life of arduousness and aridity. Nothing seems to go right
for such a one. Toxicity leaves a person out of sorts with himself or herself, out of communion with the spirit. Therefore, life never seems to
work out. Unity with the spirit helps to order situations and incidents in
such a way that life flows together; it works out; it is felt to be well
worth living.

Don't Give Up

St. Paul continues in his letter to the Colossians, "...in accordance with
His glorious strength, with all power always to persevere and endure,
giving thanks with joy to the Father who has made you able to share the
lot of God's holy people and with them to inherit the light" (Col 1:12).
The power to persevere and endure is necessary to understand God's will.
His will is not necessarily clear immediately, or once and for all. Life

must be lived in a patient and enduring manner before the true nature of His providential caring becomes apparent.

Giving in to total despair and faithlessness creates an internal climate opposed to health and spiritual well-being. Worries and fears then grab hold of the conscious mind. Rather than waging the fight of faith in order to gain the light of Christ's understanding, shining deep in the soul, one yields to hopelessness. At that point, the revelation of God's will is dammed up and may be quite a long while in coming forth.

The cure of souls calls forth an unrelenting faith in the healing power of Jesus. God's will is for healing and health. Jesus, when diligently sought, inevitably bequeaths interior wholeness which may often become manifest as physical healing.

The medical journal *Cancer* reported the case of Sylvia Bassetti. Mrs. Bassetti, age eighty, was diagnosed with cancer of the lymph nodes. For a number of months, she noticed a "pink being" lump on her neck. During this time, she also experienced numbness in her side and head and lost a significant amount of weight.

When the doctor diagnosed her cancer, Mrs. Bassetti remarked, "I didn't let it get to me. You know how people become depressed when they get cancer? Not me. I didn't grieve over it. I just went on with my life."

Mrs. Bassetti did not manifest immediately threatening symptoms. Due to the failure of traditional therapy to treat lymph node cancer, her treatment was deferred. Three months after her diagnosis, Mrs. Bassetti's cancer showed signs of complete regression. In fact, the numbness disappeared and she gained weight. Twelve years after her diagnosis, she is completely healthy and quite energetic.

In commenting on her remarkable recovery, she asserted, "I'm a religious person. I prayed a lot. So, I attribute it to my faith in God. I guess He just didn't want me to have cancer."

Of course, many factors play into healing. In the case of Bassetti, her faith maximized the healing potential of her body. We could say that it was just not her time to pass on and, therefore, she was able to effect healing via faith. She sensed God's will for her life and did not give in to toxic despair.

Despair is toxic because it throws the soul into lethargy and hopelessness. True enough, it may be quite redemptive in that it could possibly result from going the wrong way in the first place. It could be God's way of redirecting us, allowing the rug to be pulled out from under us, so to speak. A passing despair, then, washes through us. But it passes. It reorients. It calls us into transformation, change, new life.

If despair does not pass, then a person may be hiding out. In a sense, despair may be easier than freedom. With freedom and new opportunities come potential challenges and problems that must be faced and worked out. With despair, one merely sulks, hides out, and lives an infected life from an infected soul.

Perseverance makes the impossible possible. Wholeness, in opposition to toxicity, fires the flame of growth and development. However, real life, really seeking the whole and the holy, is a journey not easily trodden but plentifully full of rewards — the realizing of inner potentials.

A holy woman told the following story:

> A man was casually browsing through the market place and lo and behold, much to his surprise, he found God behind the counter of a very expensive shop. He asked God, "What's for sale here?" God replied, "Anything and everything your heart desires." This man was dumbfounded at the thought of talking to God. He could have anything he had ever dreamed of or hoped for. He quickly declared, "I want great happiness, great peace of mind, and freedom from all my fears. I want this for myself and for everyone on earth." God smiled and whispered, "You must understand, we don't sell fruits here. Only seeds."

In Him All Things Hold Together

St. Paul's letter to the Colossians reflects the psychological and spiritual fact that in Christ all inner and outer realities find their meaning. In the cure of souls, the presence of Divine energy is a frequent occurrence. The individual's inner and outer life coincide in such a way that the interior experience of grace is often manifest in a change in one's outer life. In this sense, God is neither solely inside nor outside of us. He is both inside and outside. The realization of grace in the moment, the experience of God's will for your life, is the ultimate source of all healing.

This mystery is ineffable and beyond the grasp of rational human intellect. Even the attempt to imagine the all-embracing nature of Christ literally boggles the mind. He is in all things, He created all things, and in Him all of us live, move, and have our being. Christ is the center point of the universe inwardly and outwardly.

The healing of the soul gently moves the person into this unending flow of grace. Inner harmony is witnessed through the harmonious ordering of external events. No longer does one feel separated and isolated in the midst of a vast universe. Instead, on a very intimate level, one senses a connection — a belonging to others and to the living universe. In a very uncanny way, inner and outer realities link together in Christ. He is the connecting principle governing and ordering all of life.

The coinciding of inner and outer transformation is witnessed in the life of St. Anthony:

> For as his soul was free from disturbances, his outward appearance was calm; so from the joy of his soul, he possessed a cheerful countenance, and from his bodily movement could be perceived the condition of his soul, as it is written: "When the heart is merry, the countenance is cheerful, but when it is sorrowful, it is cast down" (Prv 15:13). Thus Anthony was recognized; he was never disturbed for his soul was at peace; he was never downcast for his mind was joyous.

The Over and Over Again God

St. Paul writes in Colossians, "He is the image of the unseen God, the first-born of all creation, for in Him were created all things in heaven and on earth" (Col 1:15–16).

The human being is a living icon of the unseen God. Deep within the recesses of the human soul is the innate potential to evolve into the likeness of the Risen Jesus. Little by little, through life experiences that are humbly understood and endured, and therefore growth promoting, transformation into His likeness unfolds. All of this takes place in a hidden and quiet way. Nothing on the outside may quite betray the intensity of the inner fire and cross-bearing that results in character growth and strengthening.

Spiritual growth does not proceed in a linear fashion. Rather, we circle around and around the Son of Righteousness. Each and every circling draws us closer into Him. As planets circle about the sun, so the soul revolves around a communion with Jesus.

Over and over again we may go through certain hardships, particular trials and temptations, ever present challenges, in order that we may

learn the inner way of truth and freedom. Time after time, God calls out
for radical change in our personal life. Time after time, His grace meets
us to guide us through our stumbling learning. God gives us time, indeed a lifetime, to learn from Him. He is ever gracious and merciful.
Jesus realizes that we hardly ever learn from our first failings; we require
repeated experiences with the same difficulties before truth dawns within
us and deliverance takes hold.

Tom, a twenty-three-year-old computer programmer, remembered his
many anxious thoughts regarding his life and God's love for him. Having been raised by a very harsh and dictatorial father, Tom believed that
God ruled mercilessly over him. At one and the same time, Tom loved
God but trembled with anxious anticipation of encountering a fault-
finding father. Tom literally conceived of God as a colossal white-haired
father who recorded every little mistake in his life and would hold him
accountable for the most minor of transgressions.

After many months of psychotherapy and an intense weekend of
retreat and prayer, Tom reflected:

> I am beginning to see that God is more merciful than I have real-
> ized. Sunday morning, I wept and wept with the realization that
> not only had my father been too hard on me, but I took up where he
> left off. I'm the harsh and unforgiving person in my own life. God
> understands me. He gives me room to make mistakes and learn
> from them. I was set free this weekend. I can make mistakes, learn
> from them and grow from them. God understands and gives me
> grace and sees me through.

When you feel that you have to hold your life together, a harsh,
demanding, toxic attitude can cripple your soul. If you are responsible
for your own salvation, then all is surely lost. No one of us is able to
redeem himself or herself. Jesus, through His death and resurrection
freely imparts grace to those who earnestly seek Him within. As you
recognize the reality of this inner grace, you will also feel more understanding and compassion for yourself. Over and over again, He bestows
grace to carry you through life's lessons. Each and every situation,
occurrence, and mistake helps to form you into the image of the unseen
God. All this is accomplished through Him in whom all things hold
together.

Guidance Through Holy Happenings

Jesus guides through holy happenings. Uncanny coincidences that leave
one filled with a sense of emotion and awe often signal the presence of

God working in the soul and in the situation. Keeping this in mind, each and every unusual event calls us to pause and deliberately reflect on its potential meaning. Jesus works most naturally through the coinciding of inner grace with the coming together of outer events.

Usually, there is no way to account for unusual happenings via logic or intellectual reasoning. Holy happenings just happen. At first, they seem to come out of nowhere. Only upon reflection do we become aware of the presence of God's hidden grace. I have often felt the sense of warmth, awe, or an unfathomable wonder in the midst of such holy happenings. Without knowing why and without logical explanations, I intuitively trust the meaning and importance of these synchronous times. True, such occurrences are purely subjective and without empirical proof regarding their emergence from Divine resources. However, the individual always knows, I always know, the movement of soul that takes place while living through the holy happening.

God guides in at least three different ways when using holy happenings. First of all, events occurring at a distance that are of personal importance may intuitively become known. That is to say, without knowing how, a person is able to detect far away events. One morning during my time of prayer, I distinctly sensed the presence of my grandmother enter the room. As far as I knew, she was then at a local hospital progressing well from an illness. Upon her entering, I felt that she was coming to say goodbye.

I raised my hands and arms out toward her, blessed her, and gave her all my love as she entered into the loving embrace of Jesus for eternity. Later on that morning, I discovered that my grandmother had passed away approximately two hours after my prayer-time experience. This holy happening greatly moved my soul.

Secondly, holy happenings occur with regard to knowledge concerning future events. One morning, just prior to rising for prayer, I dreamed that one of the psychologists in my office and I would be going through a friendly divorce. Upon awakening, I had no reason to believe that there were difficulties or troubles of any sort between us. However, I knew that the dream could be preparing me for a future event. That afternoon, this same psychologist courteously asked if he could speak with me. In a very friendly manner he told me that he no longer felt himself to be interested in pursuing a profession as a psychotherapist. Instead, he desired to branch out on his own and develop a psychological testing practice. As he was telling me of his decision, the dream came to mind: a friendly divorce was taking place. God's guidance, an abundance of grace, had been provided for me through the dream — through a holy happening.

Lastly, holy happenings take place through what I have referred to earlier as God incidents, seeming coincidences that, in actuality, are moments of grace. At one point in our lives, Kathy and I were going through a particularly trying set of circumstances. We were both experiencing a great deal of interior pain and growth. During a morning conversation, she said, "I feel that you and I and the children are on an ark, just like Noah and his family. It's storming and raining outside, but it's alright, we are going to make it."

Shortly after our conversation, our daughter, Katherine, walked into our bedroom and informed us of her dream. That evening our seven-year-old daughter dreamed that all of us, as a family, were on an ark together, "just like Noah's ark." Flabbergasted, Kathy and I looked at each other. This holy happening confirmed God's guidance and the movement of His grace in our lives. In point of fact, we came through our ordeal safe and sound, as individuals and as a family.

Thus, St. Paul's declaration to the Colossians that, "In Him all things hold together" bestows a plenitude of meaning for all of us. The future, with all of its challenges and potentials, is known by Him, and He bequeaths grace to us in order to deal with these upcoming events. Events occurring at a distance are also known by Him, and, in accord with the graciousness of His caring, He imparts grace to the soul that aids in knowing about and dealing with distant matters. Even at this very moment in time, His will is being made clear through ostensibly coincidental, God incidental, happenings.

The minister of healing need only cooperate with this flow of grace. The full realization that the grace of Jesus transcends time, space, and distance enables the minister to greatly trust the working of Providence during the course of healing. With adequate time, patience, and the coming together of various events, inner and outer healing occurs. Never to be rushed or hurried, the grace of healing moves in His time and in His way. The healer learns to cooperate and assist his or her patient to also yield to healing grace.

Daily life abounds with instances of God's will and personal feeling. At just the right moment in time, events come together in an uncanny manner to meet the need at hand. No amount of conscious contrivance can create such a miraculous pulling together of people, events, and timing. At the moment when all seems lost, the ego is most profoundly yielded to Divine guidance. At the point of our greatest humbling, we acutely see that, "In Him all things hold together."

God Sees You Through Thick and Thin

God's will for your life is to see you through thick and thin as you begin and end in Him. To see us through thick and thin suggests that life does indeed have its ups and downs. Difficult times and easy times are the lot of humankind. On any given day, we feel a mixture of positive and negative emotions. Never can we expect to experience completely smooth sailing.

Beginning and ending in Jesus calls us to remain completely focused on Him regardless of the ups and downs, the thick and thin of life. In Jesus, ups can be ups and downs can be downs as long as one remains steadfast in seeking and growing in Him. Without such unwavering determination, ups take us up too high and downs pull us down too low. Often our trust can be in good feelings or in bad feelings rather than in Jesus. The beginning and ending of all things is in Him and, therefore, we can move forward courageously knowing that He is our source and our goal.

Energized in Jesus

St. Paul asserts, "And it is for this reason that I labor, striving with His energy which works in me mightily" (Col 1:29). The only way to adequately discern God's will is to be energized by Him. Clarity of mind regarding God's purpose for everyday life does not make itself known in the majority of situations. More likely, an ever-present energy is required to live life daily, step by step, trusting that He will make His guidance plain.

Such energy results from Divine infilling rather than human contrivance. One who is truly led by the Spirit moves with an ever-steady anointing of energy and freshness. An individual who pushes and induces, in a forced manner, contact with God, lives a life of severe ups and downs. Human energy, rather than holy energy, motivates such a one. A numinous prompting and outpouring of the Holy Spirit always leads into emotional depth and stability rather than into flight and strain. The energy of Jesus flows relatively unimpeded in one who from the heart seeks His will.

Rooted in Jesus

St. Paul continues, "So then, as you received Jesus as Lord and Christ, now live your lives in Him, be rooted in Him and built upon Him, held firm by the faith you have been taught, and overflowing with thanksgiving" (Col 2:6–7).

An infusion of energy without rootedness quickly evaporates. One who feels wild-eyed with excitement and spiritual vigor must be cautious lest an inauthentic spiritual movement be accepted. When Jesus moves, He moves with surety and depth, quite different from fleeting human excitement. The energy of Jesus always flows with rootedness in Jesus.

Rootedness can be discerned by at least three signs: a greater desire for prayer, an increased understanding of one's neighbor, and a more intense and consistent self-reflection. A soul energized with the love of Jesus feels drawn to Jesus in the quietness and depth of personal prayer. Together with this, others are loved, understood, and accepted more readily. A self-reflection that allows interior darkness to surface into the healing light of Christ on a daily basis also accompanies the sense of being energized and rooted in Jesus.

For one called by ministry, by profession, indeed by life, into the cure of souls, the true movement of God's spirit within can thus be discerned in the fruits of prayer, love, and self-reflection. The psychotherapist, the minister, the friend, can fully trust apparent transformations of soul that manifest these fruits. Christ Jesus, glorified as Lord, reigns supreme in the heart of one who diligently seeks His will without being seduced by human excitement or being led astray by fleeting impulses. A relationship of healing in which two individuals agree to journey together in search of the pearl of great price always discovers Jesus Who is to be found by those who diligently search for Him with a firmness of faith and an unrelenting devotion.

God's Touch Afresh

God's will brings a fresh touch. Walking in the will of Jesus creates a smooth pathway through life. True, ups and downs are inevitable but He is the one who smooths down the mountains and fills in the valleys. With a fresh touch from Him, new courage and surety motivate the believer.

The wondrous poem of Gerard Manley Hopkins entitled "The Wreck of the Deutschland" eloquently describes this fresh touch:

Thou mastering me
God! giver of breath and bread;
Worlds strand, sway of the sea;
Lord of living and dead;
Thou hast bound bones and veins in me,
fastened me flesh,
And after it almost unmade, what with dread,
Thy doing: and thus thou touch me afresh?
Over again I feel thy finger and find thee.

Changed Heart — Changed Circumstances

Since you have been raised up to be with Christ, you must look for
the things that are above, where Christ is, sitting at God's right
hand. Let your thoughts be on things above, not on the things
that are in the earth, because you have died, and now the life you
have is hidden with Christ in God. But when Christ is revealed —
and He is your life — you too, will be revealed with Him in glory.
(Col 3:1–4)

Setting one's heart on Christ directs us to an inner constancy of focus.
Inner realities determine outer realities. As interior vision is maintained
on Christ, so outer circumstances change accordingly. The life that
springs up within the soul nourishes and orders outer events and circumstances.

In fact, a changed heart draws changed circumstances. Usually, that
which we experience in the external world in some way reflects our
interior state of being. We project toxic disharmony and chaos into the
outer world and experience it as perplexing dilemmas, constant conflict,
and misunderstanding after misunderstanding. On the other hand, interior
harmony also is projected into the outer world and, as a matter of conse-
quence, the situation and people drawn into one's life are more stable,
tranquil, and positive.

I remember a young woman complaining about being able to find
only angry and abusive men to date. In her words, "All men are hurtful.
I'll never find anyone really to love me." In reality, she always ended up
with verbally and even physically abusive men.

After some months in psychotherapy, we became aware of her very
hidden rage directed against herself. She believed that she deserved to be
mistreated and even abused. Unconsciously, she sought out such individuals and predicaments.

After approximately a year and a half of intensive psychotherapy, her interior state had changed remarkably. One evening, after finishing some work at her local parish, she locked the front door of the church and turned to walk to her car. In the parking lot she saw a very distressed man whose car would not start. As she approached him, she recognized him! He was her dentist. He had, unfortunately, forgotten to turn off his headlights. After Mass, he discovered that his battery was dead. Fortunately, she stored jumper cables in her car's trunk, and offered them to him. Soon his automobile battery was recharged. He was a single man and knew that she also was unattached. Out of gratitude, he asked her out for a hamburger. Ten months later, they were preparing for marriage. A new man came her way once she had cleared through old and destructive inner attitudes that prevented goodness and health from entering into her life.

She knew God's fresh touch firsthand. Thoughtfully, she reflected, "I could not see the reality of this truth before. What is on the inside of me always showed up on the outside of me. A new heart gave me new opportunities and possibilities for living a healthy and creative life."

Harmony

Knowing God's will for your life always involves yielding to harmony. Life is a force of harmonious exchange, of give and take between individuals, groups of people, and the times and seasons of life. In due course, God's will always unfolds through a harmonious coming together of life forces.

One who runs counter to God's will experiences a grinding quality of going against the grain. Such a one walks against the current of a powerfully flowing river. To move against God's spirit produces interior unsettledness and outer chaos. When things just don't seem to come together, this signals a misalignment regarding God's will.

An interior prompting that causes one to feel that he or she is possibly being led by God into this or that action is always confirmed by a synchronous flow of events. In other words, living in God's will creates the interior sensation of flowing with the river of life. One perceives that a force bigger than oneself is in control and, in a very hidden manner, anticipating and ordering all that is meant to be. God's will is a will of free-flowing order and harmony.

A healthy life bespeaks a fusion between the Divine and the human. A blessed saint wrote:

Jesus has come to take up his abode in my heart. It is not so much a habitation, an association, as a sort of fusion. Oh, new and blessed life! life which becomes each day more luminous....The wall before me, dark a few moments since, is splendid at this hour because the sun shines on it. Wherever its gaze falls, they light up a conflagration of glory; the smallest speck of glass sparkles, each grain of sand in its fire; even so, there is a royal song of triumph in my heart because the Lord is there. My days succeed each other; yesterday a blue sky; to-day a clouded sun; a night filled with strange dreams; but as soon as the eyes open, and I regain consciousness and seem to begin life again, it is always the same figure before me, always the same presence filling my heart.... Formerly, the day was dulled by the absence of the Lord. I used to wake, invaded by all sorts of sad impressions, and I did not find Him on my path. To-day, He is with me; and the light cloudiness which covers things is not an obstacle to my communion with Him. I feel the pressure of His hand, I feel something else which fills me with a serene joy; shall I dare to speak it out? Yes, for it is the true expression of what I experience. The Holy Spirit is not merely making me a visit; it is no mere dazzling apparition which may from one moment to another spread its wings and leave me in my night. It is a permanent habitation. He can depart only if He takes me with Him. More than that; He is not other than myself: He is one with me. It is not a juxtaposition, it is a penetration, a profound modification of my nature, a new manner of my being.

Live Life

St. Paul encouragingly writes, "There is only Christ: He is everything and He is in everything" (Col 3:11). Life is Christ and Christ is Life. He is the only and ultimate reality.

Christ Jesus fills everything and is in everything. Nothing could exist without the life force of Jesus abiding within it. Without Him, the entire universe ceases to exist. With Him, all that is thrives with on-going vitality.

This understanding enables us to approach life confidently, beckons us to live life. A dualistic mentality maintains that forces of good and forces of evil battle against each other with equal power. This kind of logic asserts that either good or evil will win out, depending on some unknown and threatening factors. Simply put, this notion asserts that the devil is ready to pounce on the soul and possess it at any given moment. Therefore, a believer trapped in dualistic thinking approaches life fearfully and very constrictedly. Life is feared, not lived.

St. Paul, I believe, urges us to consider a more unitive way of living. The only and ultimate reality is Christ. Evil does exist. But the life of Christ far supercedes and overcomes the threat of evil. In a manner of speaking, the devil is a toothless lion. One who abides deeply in God knows that Jesus permeates every situation, every relationship, and every difficulty. For the moment, toxic evil may seem to have the upper hand, but with steadfastness, acquired through the understanding of Christ being in everything, the providential working of grace inevitably surfaces.

No problem, no matter how big, can thwart the creative and redemptive life of Christ. All things turn toward Him eventually and definitely. This is the unity of life. We need have no fear with the understanding that Christ is everything and is in everything.

A dear friend of mine had acquired the maiming habit of smoking. For many years I wondered how such a spiritual man could continue this unhealthy behavior. I even asked him once and he jokingly responded, "God isn't finished with me yet." Kathy and I visited him one summer in Chicago. He had recently suffered the trauma of a severe automobile accident that left him with a broken arm. During our conversation, he, Kathy, and I were filled with the satisfaction of shared insights and experiences. I soon noticed that he was no longer smoking. When I commented on this, he readily replied, "The accident shook me up and, in the process, shook the cigarettes out of my hand. God was present in my accident. He saved my life. Through this trauma, I have learned a great deal. I no longer need those cigarettes. I need only Him."

The living of life brings with it grace for growth. Life, lived fully and not fearfully, breathes with the ever-present will of God. His voice can be heard in every situation and difficulty for one who has ears to hear. Since He is in everything, in every toxic life predicament, our call is to deliberately and confidently live life.

Live Peace

A harmonious way of life calls forth not only the confidence to be about the business of living life fully, but also creates a new ability to live peace. By this, I mean that one notices that peace becomes a way of life rather than a passing emotion. The more immersed we are in God's will, the more we are able to savor a life of peace.

St. Paul attempted to cultivate this life of peace in the heart of believers as he wrote, "And may the peace of Christ reign in your hearts, because it is for this that you are called together in one body. Always be thankful" (Col 3:15). As peace reigns within the heart, life takes on a harmonious accord with the will of God. His will becomes our will and our will His will. In truth, peace reigns in the heart of one who experientially lives out the will of God as a matter of course, as easily as drawing in the next breath.

I have noticed that living peace is far easier as one becomes acquainted with the seasons of life. The sacred scriptures note, "There is a season for everything, a time for every occupation under heaven; a time for giving birth, a time for dying; a time for planting, a time for uprooting that which has been planted, a time for killing, a time for healing" (Eccl 3:1–3).

If the seasons of life are ignored, avoided, or denied, then unsettledness of soul can plague an individual. Things will not seem to come together. Often, such a one feels like he or she is going against the grain of life. In a very real sense, we battle against life itself when we refuse to admit the changes in our life.

Oftentimes, life requires us to move into a time of introversion when we have been used to living in an extroverted manner. As we grow older, this is often the case. Rather than being so concerned about a great many outer activities and events, one is called to live a deeper life of reflection, contemplation, and the interior experience of the Holy. If such a call is refused, then crises seem to bombard one's life. Physical illness, financial predicaments, marital and family discord may all thwart the person who is going against God's inspiration. God's will is a will of harmony, a will that guides us to live peace — not disaster, discord, or confusion.

Recently, my wife and I attended the twenty-fifth anniversary celebration to the Catholic priesthood of a friend of ours. Walking by crowds of people, Kathy and I started conversing with different folks. I greeted a number of friends I had not seen in a long while. I turned and noticed Kathy speaking with two female friends who were university professors. As I watched her, a feeling of unease came over me.

Without knowing why, I felt strangely out of sorts. When Kathy questioned my sudden remoteness and agitation, I replied that I was fine. Indeed, I was not conscious of any troublesome concern. Not until the next day did I come to grips with the source of my interior disharmony.

Over dinner that evening, I confided to Kathy:

I really was distressed yesterday. When I saw you talking to those two professors, the future seemed to pass before my eyes. I felt with some certainty that someday you would achieve your Ph.D. Perhaps you would teach literature or religious studies at a university. You would meet so many new people, so many interesting men. Maybe, you would meet someone more interesting or attractive than I. Would you still love me once you had made your mark in the world?

Kathy gently assured me with her understanding:

I always feel that way when you are traveling and giving retreats or conferences. A silly thought passes through my mind. I wonder if you would fall in love with someone else or someone else would fall in love with you. It is my own insecurity that surfaces every time you leave. When you return and I see you at the airport, our eyes meet and I realize the foolishness of my worries. Over time, those insecurities have lessened and lessened. I know that you love me. And I love you.

As I had reflected on the changing seasons of life in my relationship with Kathy, I had momentarily felt quite insecure, as though I wanted to forcefully block changes from occurring in our relationship. This egocentric impulse took hold of me in a moment's time — a sure sign of moving against the grain of life, against the inevitable seasons of life. With depth of understanding, facing my own egocentric inclination, I felt restored to inner equanimity, balance and harmony.

Let It Be and Expect a Miracle

To understand the nature of God's will for your life requires a two-fold commitment: the willingness to let the present situation be, and the certitude of, at the same time, expecting a miracle. A complete resignation to God's will, letting it be, creates an attitude of receptivity in the soul. Rather than forcing the hand of God, so to speak, the individual acknowledges the reality of the present situation and then yields himself or herself to faith in God. Thus, the ego does not intrude but cooperates. God is grace then set free to work, often in miraculous ways.

Kathy and I were recently teaching on this subject. Prior to this, she had written a wonderful article entitled "Let It Be" for the quarterly newsletter published by Christian Psychological Foundation. With her permission, I would like to share with you her insights:

> "Do not fret....Trust in the Lord and do good, dwell in the land and enjoy safe pasture. Delight yourself in the Lord and He will give you the desires of your heart" (Ps 37:1–4).
>
> Changes are inevitable in life. With change comes a variety of feelings, fretfulness being one of them. No matter how potentially wonderful a change may be, it is still the death of an old and somewhat cherished way of life. No matter how frightening and devastating a change may seem, it can, in the long run, bring great fruitfulness.
>
> Some years bring more change than others, and it has been in this year that I have seen more profound changes in my life than in the years past. In traveling and speaking with my husband, Paul, and in my involvement with the Foundation, I have found that the primary concerns of people, in general, are those of being loved and feeling self-worth. Surprisingly, I found myself having these same concerns. I was doing a great deal of fretting.
>
> During one of these "fretting moods," I worried over questions such as, "Am I being a good wife and mother? What does so and so think of me? How can I change this or that situation?" During prayer, the thought came to me, "Let it be." I realized that I had been spending a great deal of time trying to change myself and situations that were not under my control. I had to learn to "Let it be," to go about my daily business without worry. What is utmost in my mind now is not what others think about me, but what I think about myself, and more importantly, what God thinks about me.
>
> I am reminded of one Miryam of Judah (the Hebrew name for the mother of Jesus), who knew how to "Let it be," who knew how to let go and let God be God.

The art of letting things be takes a lifetime to develop. As we learn more and more, so we grow more and more in tune with God's will for our own life. Without toxic anxiety, we trust in Him. Doing all that we can do and then, confidently, we trust in Him, is what "letting it be" is all about. Once anxious striving, insensitive ambition, and burnout are experienced, the soul has surely departed from this receptive stance. "Letting it be" soothes, settles, and disposes the soul to providential intervention and sustenance.

Follow Your Heart

"May the words of my mouth always find favor, and the whisperings of my heart, in your presence, Yahweh, my rock, my redeemer" (Ps 19:14).

In the human heart, God speaks. He whispers words of understanding and we, in turn, whisper words of love, concern, or desire. Heart whispers to heart and in this, God's will is discerned.

To follow your heart means to follow the whisperings heard therein. These gentle nudges and encouraging words lead us to fully embrace life while, at the same time, yearning for more and more of God. To follow the heart means to always listen, to always acknowledge both doubts and inspirations and to always proceed with faith. At times, His whisperings are unmistakably clear. For the most part, however, we do our best and still then hear only faintly. No matter how dimly or brightly the heavenly word comes forth from within, it must be acted upon with faith — a heartfelt desire to be true to one's own self and, therein, true to Christ Jesus.

At times, spirits other than God's spirit might speak. The whisperings of fear, for instance, frequently plague the soul. Fear prompts the individual to act impulsively, wildly, from a position of either frightened withdrawal or an inflated desire to prove one's self. The telling point is whether or not one senses anxiety. The voice of fear always injects toxic anxiety into the person. This unruly tension causes one to withdraw out of fright or to over-exert oneself in order to compensate for the fear. The voice of fear is different than the voice of Christ Jesus within.

The spirit of zealotry also can wreak havoc and be confused with God's guidance. In spiritual matters, one can feel interiorly prompted to be quite zealous, dominating, and exclusive. Ambition of this sort segregates and divides people. A pecking order develops in groups that are motivated by ambition. Usually, the most zealous person in the group calls others to follow his or her "pastoral leadership" with a rather blind allegiance. In a similar manner, spiritually zealous parents force their faith on their children. Rather than having the best interests of the children in mind, the parents instead are motivated by what others will think. They want to have and be known as having a spiritual family. More frequently than not, this serves to drive children away from the faith since their own personhood has been violated.

To follow Jesus from the heart supremely insures the worth and dignity of the individual. Jesus speaks directly to the unique and personal need of each man and woman. All He asks is that one struggles humbly to hear His whisperings in the heart and more and more discern His will. T. S. Elliot poignantly reflected:

> There are only hints and guesses.
> Hints followed by guesses; and the rest
> Is prayer, observance, discipline, thought and action.

Toxicity and God's Will

The more the soul emerges out of toxic relationship, the more God's will can be discerned. In fact, the experience of toxicity is a sure sign that one is out of touch with God's will. The only exception to this is in the working through of toxicity. Toxicity must be experienced in order to be healed. In so far as it is part of the healing process, the feeling of toxicity can be said to be a part of God's will for your life. But, the ultimate will of God is to discover healing and release from toxicity.

I have frequently observed that the toxic reaction incurred by living outside of God's will causes people to feel as though they have "stepped into a bad space." That is to say, a spiritual space of confusion, discord, and anxiety has been entered. It is much like the shock one would experience by finding oneself thrown into a completely foreign country where nothing is familiar and everything feels confusing. This is not referring to the sort of disorientation then that can accompany healthy spiritual growth and change. It is instead a discordant and disintegrating experience of toxicity.

A young man who had been involved with a very rigid and fundamentalist prayer group felt, as the result of his intensive work in psychotherapy, that he must leave the gathering. He noticed that the prayer meetings left him ill at ease and out of touch with God's presence. He would not feel inwardly settled for days after attending this very extroverted and superficial "spiritual" meeting. After not having attended these weekly gatherings for a number of months, he decided to visit the group once again, out of a desire to see old friends, because, "after all, it couldn't be that bad."

Quite often during intensive inner-transformation, an individual questions his or her interior feelings and discernment. The outer situation can seem to be so innocent and benign but one's innermost feelings discern unhealth and toxicity. In such a case, it behooves the individual to maintain an interior fidelity to soul rather than acquiescing to the world of appearances. This young man acquiesced, went back to the group, one last time.

The very evening after the prayer group met, he found himself in the throes of nightmare after nightmare during his sleep. He had a horrible week at work. Interiorly he was anxious and distraught. This was a toxic reaction to a toxic situation. He had stepped out of God's will and stepped into a "bad spiritual space."

After approximately ten days and two psychotherapy sessions, he regained his quietude of soul. Toxicity had been processed out of him. He understood that he could no longer casually expose himself to chaotic and superficial situations no matter how spiritual they seemed to be. The world of appearances, what seems to be right, can be quite different from God's actual will. Only by moving into the depths of his soul, regaining contact with his innermost feelings, could he be cleansed of emotional and spiritual poisons and recenter himself in the living presence of Jesus.

Four

A New Wind Blowing

God's spirit blows where it will. No human being can direct the course of grace; only God, in and through His providential caring, moves freely and unabashedly with presence and anointing to set burdened hearts free. The purpose of an outpouring of the Holy Spirit is to liberate the oppressed and bring new life to the dying. Those who know spiritual death and decay can find new life in a new outpouring of the Holy Spirit that is beginning to emerge more and more definitely as we approach the millennium.

The time of the Old Testament emphasizes the workings of the Father. The last two thousand years clearly rang through and through with the presence of Jesus. I believe that in our day and age we are moving into an era of the Holy Spirit in which each man and woman will know God for himself or herself, will experientially have a personal relationship with Jesus who resides in the depths of the soul. Such a spirituality will generate transformation from the inside out. People's lives will be changed as their souls have been touched. A new era, a time of the Holy Ghost and fire, is ready to sweep across the face of the earth and into the hearts of men and women everywhere.

As this new wind blows Christian faith will become an intensely personal faith. The outward structures and institutions that have acted as vehicles for the expression of faith will also undergo radical changes. That which most effectively nurtures the faith experience of the individual will remain; that which no longer imparts inspiration and a touch of the holy will be swept away. The new wind is a wind of the Holy Spirit blowing freely and freshly in the human heart.

Church will become a gathering of believers who share a commonality of spirit — a common experience and expression of the inner experience of the Lord Jesus. In this, soul will be knit to soul in a life-changing and healthy manner while still retaining personal freedom, individuals will encourage and support one another in their intense walk of faith. Those who have been touched by the wind, the breath of the Spirit, will be drawn to others who have been also touched. The church will be more and more formed and inspired by the new wind blowing.

A Ton of Trouble — A Touch of Glory

The touch of Jesus can transform a ton of trouble into a touch of glory. Life's many troubles often motivate people to seek out and discover God. In fact, it can often be said that there is nothing like a crisis to bring one to God. When everything seems so out of control and overwhelming, the old, egocentric ego longs for something or someone greater than itself to provide a way through the problem. This someone is God and the only way to know Him is to allow Him to touch you with His glory.

After teaching on this topic one evening, a young man approached me and commented:

> I believe that God's spirit is indeed being poured out in a new and fresh way. What concerns me is that where grace comes in evil also seems to follow quickly on its heels. In other words, people are going to be able to have more of the Holy Spirit if they desire him but the world is also going to suffer from more problems than it has experienced to date. I guess God knows that we need more of Him for a world that will be filled with more problems.

I have often reflected on this matter and realize that as we enter into a more and more technologically sophisticated age, men and women hunger for something deeper. Advances in science are necessary and important for the betterment of humankind. Together with this, the soul yearns for a deeper nourishment and replenishment. The soul yearns to encounter the living Christ.

Without the spiritual dimension in life, one withers up and becomes depressed. Lives are filled with emptiness and a sense of meaninglessness. Without spiritual roots, highly developed technological advancements fall flat. On the other hand, an age known for incredible scientific progress will rest on solid ground as it is also remembered as an era of potently transforming spirituality.

Only the healing touch of Jesus of Nazareth can transform a ton of trouble into a touch of glory. An encounter with this presence brings forth vitality into a stale soul. One dominated by detachment, logic, and hardness becomes more relational, intuitive, and receptive. A person troubled by insurmountable problems suddenly feels hopeful when touched by His presence.

St. Paul in his first letter to the Thessalonians, emphasizes the coming presence of Christ. He writes of the *Parousia*, literally translated, presence. Just as Jesus physically came into this world, so His presence is meant to be borne more and more in the hearts of men and women. Just as humans undergo biological evolution, so the psyche evolves. In this era of the Holy Spirit the presence of Jesus comes with new vitality creating greater consciousness. To be aware of Jesus living in the soul is the most life-giving experience of all. In this is true consciousness attained.

So often I see a great many people searching for altered states of mind. They want to expand their horizons, see things in a different way, find truth. No matter how great the objective, real consciousness can be known only through the encounter with the Risen Christ. Mind altering drugs, intensive interpersonal encounters done for their own sake, ego inspired heroic feats, or any other such endeavors prove fruitless since they assuredly spring from egocentric impulses. In other words, people want God without paying the price.

To encounter God means to die to egocentricity. As one undergoes interior purgation, cleansing old and selfish attitudes, God visits the soul. The pain of such a process scares many away. For this reason, many are called but few are chosen. The journey to God is indeed quite arduous at times since it requires the daily carrying of the cross. However, this day-to-day dying to egocentricity always bears the fruit of increased interior peace and fulfillment. Bearing the cross of daily life leads one not only to Calvary but to newness of life.

So often we have entertained misconceptions with regard to interior purification and knowledge of God. In the Catholic Church for instance, we emphasize the importance of confession. Regular believers were to confess their sins and thus find immediate reconciliation to God. Sadly enough, this sacrament was often ritualized so that Catholics no longer knew its real meaning or felt its effect. It ceased to impart real presence because its meaning had been lost.

Catholics suffered under the weight of continually facing their same old problems and confessing these very same concerns week after week. No resolution was forthcoming. No relief was felt for long. Indeed, the sacrament was taken only to keep oneself out of hell and increase the likelihood of going to heaven.

I remember during my elementary school years, hearing a group of high school boys talking about their anticipated adventures Saturday night. Knowing that they had to go to confession Saturday afternoon so that they could receive communion Sunday morning, they made a decision to go to confession Saturday afternoon and list off all the sins they would commit Saturday evening. Many of them even threw in a few extra sins for good measure "just in case." They had all of their sins confessed beforehand, forgiven in advance, leaving them completely free to do as they pleased Saturday evening and receive communion Sunday morning.

How often we have thought in a similar manner. Engaging in the external observances of faith we somehow have considered to be sufficient to ensure an authentic spirituality. However, we must realize giving lip service to God keeps the soul far from Him. Acts of faith must be heartfelt in order to effect transformation.

Fortunately, I find that in contemporary society more and more heartfelt faith is to be found. Catholics are partaking of sacraments more frequently out of sincere personal devotion. The outer observance is becoming a reflection of interior inspiration. The *Parousia* is beginning.

Inspiration and Transformation

St. Paul writes to the Thessalonians: "We always thank God for you all, mentioning you in our prayers continually. We remember before our God and father how active is the faith, how unsparing the love, how persevering the hope which you have from our Lord Jesus Christ" (Ths 1:2–4). Faith, love, and hope characterize the inspired soul. An active faith enables one to deliberately trust in God for day-to-day solutions and provisions. An unsparing love looks to understand all manner of situations and predicaments as the unfolding mystery of God's work. A persevering hope causes us to never give up believing in the fidelity of God to meet our every need. The inspiration of faith, love, and hope works a gradual transformation of character in the believing soul. Such a development proceeds slowly but surely. Real healing is a matter of time, patience, and steadfastness. In the midst of ups and downs, God is always at work bringing light into the dark places of the soul and thereby effecting transformation. Thus, transformation of personality is generated by God's life-giving spirit and only by His spirit.

I have had church leaders tell me that even though their congregation members or parishioners are very external in their approach to God, it is at least better than having no faith at all. This rationale asserts that an external form of religion is preferred to a purely "secular" lifestyle. The fallacy in this lies in considering that God is also available when we approach Him externally and superficially. The fact of the matter is that the living presence of Jesus is felt only in the depths and only by going to the depths.

Without depth of faith, people are prone toward inflation and defla-
tion. Commonly we notice individuals "getting high on God" after an
intensive, externally oriented, worship service or conference. Inevitably,
depression follows this inflated experience. The weekend may have
sounded like God, seemed like God, but in fact God was not present.
How easy it is to confuse an experience of the Holy Spirit with an
encounter resulting in emotional outbursts, tears, and even groanings for
God. Whatever takes a person up high and then lets him down with a
depressive thud, perhaps a few hours or days later, is indeed inspired not
by the Holy Spirit but by other spirits.

A sincere believer attested, "God is touching me in a new way. He
is calling me to greater silence and contemplation. After so many years
of loud doing this and that for God, I'm finally settling down and living
with God. I feel better physically, emotionally, and spiritually. God is
doing a new thing in my life."

Move On with God

In a recent teaching I asserted, "You've got to move on with God if
you're going to move on." In saying this, I reflected on the fact that God
alone causes personal growth. He alone moves the soul to greater development. He alone provides grace to see one through the darkness. He
alone is a soul mover.

The cure of souls depends on God's willingness to move at the right
time with the right grace. Without God all the psychotherapy in the
world would prove fruitless, all attempts of healing of any sort would
end without effect, nothing could ever be counted on to work on behalf
of the individual. When a person does all that is humanly possible and
then trusts in God, mysterious forces seem to emerge on behalf of the
seeker. His spirit moves with healing, the wind of the Holy Spirit blows
where it will, making healing and wholeness available to the open heart.
To move on with God allows one to feel cured within day by day in a
very gradual and life-giving process.

In former days, the hierarchy of the church mediated the "cure." In
many denominations the priests, pastors, clerical hierarchy all imparted
God's blessings to an uneducated and ostensibly uninspired people. In a
manner of speaking, the spiritually poverty stricken throngs of
humankind waited as the institution deemed when the appropriate time
would be to dole out blessings. For the sake of their salvation, the

masses heeded institutional rules and rigidity. Now, in the place of institutional domination, a new wind imparts blessings to every living person. Through such an intimate experience with Jesus, knowing Him personally and assuredly, the soul grows and is cured.

The story is told of the pious Jew who felt deeply troubled by the observance of the Sabbath, the Day of the Lord. Originally this day was considered a time of great joy, but rabbis continued issuing one rule and regulation after another regarding how the Sabbath was to be observed. Some Jews trembled with fear lest they transgress one regulation or another on the Sabbath.

One night God provided the pious Jew with grace in the form of a dream. An angel carried him off to heaven and showed him two thrones. The Jew asked, "For whom are these reserved?" The angel replied, "For you as long as you live your life in God; and for a man whose name and address will be given to you."

The pious fellow was then taken by the angel to a horrible and dark spot in hell. Indeed it was by far the most damned of quarters in the infernal prison. He asked, "And who is to live here?" The angel replied, "You if you do not live in God and for the man whose name and address are being written down for you."

As the dream continued, the pious Jew visited the man who was to be his companion in heaven. This fellow lived among the gentiles. On the Sabbath he gave a banquet filled with merrymaking and laughter. The pious Jew approached the fellow and asked why he held this banquet on the Sabbath. The man answered, "During the years of my childhood, my parents instructed me that the Sabbath was a day of rest and rejoicing. On Saturdays my mother made the most delicious meals, we laughed and danced with family and friends. I do the same to this very day."

The pious Jew quickly attempted to instruct this man with regard to the rules and regulations concerning the Sabbath. However, an angel quickly struck the Jew dumb. At that moment, he realized that this man's spiritual joy in the Sabbath would be sapped away if he were made to feel guilty by the rabbis' rules.

The pious Jew was then taken by the angel to the home of the man who was to be his companion in hell. He found that this man was a strict observer of the rabbis' rules and regulations. Every Sabbath day this man was fraught with tension and worry lest he depart from the ironclad rules governing the Sabbath. The pious Jew thought about remonstrating him for his slavery to the law. But he quickly realized that the man would never understand how he could stray from God by obeying religious rules.

When the pious Jew awoke from his dream, he knew that to live in God is a matter not of following external rules and regulations but of living in God wholeheartedly and joyfully.

Note: The Quest for the Mysterium

In St. Paul's first letter to the Thessalonians, he repeatedly stresses his allegiance to God rather than to man: "...nor have we ever looked for honor from human beings, either from you or anybody else, when we could have imposed ourselves on you with full weight, as apostles of Christ" (1 Ths 2:6–7). St. Paul adamantly refused to permit concerns for human admiration to interfere with his single-hearted devotion to God's will. He moved in his life only as God bid him to move and not out of a desire for human approval.

St. Paul continues, "Another reason why we continually thank God for you is that as soon as you heard the word that we brought you as God's message, you welcomed it for what it really is, not the word of any human being, but God's word, a power that is working among you believers" (Ths 1:2–13). In turning away from seeking after human recognition, an individual, as reflected in St. Paul's writings, began the search for God's power working within — the Mysterium. This sense of God's interior presence calls the believer to greater growth and individuality. God's life force operating within the soul is a power that works when it wills and where it wills. That is to say, no person has the ability to manipulate God's power working within him or her. Our only aptitude as human beings lies in cooperating with God's power at work within us.

The Mysterium has a magnetic quality that draws the soul to itself. Jesus is a jealous God and wants us for Himself alone. His love compels us toward Him. Once we have tasted His presence, nothing else can ever replace it.

At a national conference on Christian psychology, a man stood up during morning prayer and thanked God for calling him to the profession and ministry of Christian psychology. Before entering the field of Christian psychology he had been employed as an engineer. After undergoing his own psychotherapy and encountering Jesus in the depths of his own soul, he felt an inspiration to enter the field of Christian psychology. In his words:

I needed to drink more deeply of the mystery of Christ in me. As I pursued my studies and later on through my professional work, I have come to know Him — the mystery — more wondrously than ever before. Through the grace of God my life is now devoted to the mystery of Christ in me, Jesus who brings healing and wholeness to hurting hearts.

Jesus, who is always at work within the heart of the believer, enables one to transcend the mundane quality of everyday life into the realization of the mystery of everyday life. In so doing, life becomes packed with meaning to be explored and understood. Each event of life carries the seed of God's unfolding plan. Encountering this mystery provides new meaning for the individual and thus imparts healing for everyday hurts and pains.

Once the mystery of the kingdom within has been experienced, the desire for it grows. Anything short of the mystery of Christ leaves one high and dry. He and He alone is sought faithfully and daily. In so doing an inner equanimity and balance pervades the soul. Emotional stability and health characterize one who is centered on God.

Being out of balance, out of touch with Christ within, unsettles the soul and creates a feeling of being "out of sorts." Usually anger results. A young man told me:

> After a very profound experience of Jesus within me, I had to make certain changes in my life. For one, I had to let my heavy drinking buddies in our local church group know that I wouldn't be available to be president of the organization any longer. The night of our regular meeting and poker party was the same night of the small prayer meeting in our parish. I couldn't do both.
>
> The night that I told them, all the guys really got on my case. The small prayer group of twenty or twenty-five people was largely composed of women. A couple of guys made fun of me for going off and praying with the women. They jeered that somehow I felt I was better than all of them. I told them that they were still my friends but I had to do what I had to do. God took on a whole new meaning for me and not even my friends could hold me back from spending time with Him. I encouraged them to come on over and give it a try, to pray with us, to experience Jesus firsthand. They just laughed and told me that maybe one of these days they'd give it a try.
>
> I felt better after I was honest with my buddies. The whole week before talking with them I was irritable and out of sorts at

home. My wife and I had fought a number of times during that week which is very unusual for us. I was caught between my old way of life and following God in a new way. Until I made up my mind to go on with God, I sure felt out of sorts and angry all the time. Once I did what I had to do and talked with my friends, I settled down and felt at peace again. My life is moving on with God.

Personally, I have found that the quest for the Mysterium grew more and more real and intense as I sought God. During my teenage years, I experienced a very life-changing spiritual encounter. For me, I truly came to know Jesus. In the midst of shared prayer with a group of five or six musician friends, I asked Jesus to become Lord of my life. I surrendered my heart to Jesus. At that very moment in time and space He came to me, I went to Him, or both. We met. Jesus became intimate and personal in my life.

This experience with the Divine opened me up to the spiritual world. More and more earnestly I sought after a deeper knowledge of Him. Institutional religion helped at times but could also prove quite limiting. Various movements within the church provided some inspiration but often I found myself distracted by various forms of mob psychology at work. I hungered for more of Jesus — pure Jesus.

A life crisis urged me into analysis. Through much soul searching and increase in self-knowledge, I slowly felt the mystery of Jesus within me more and more. As I continued to walk this inner walk, I prayed daily for the grace to walk humbly with Him through the course of my life. I found the mystery of Jesus seems to be ever unfolding. My soul has felt the cure that happens and continues to happen as I move along with the new wind blowing.

Passion for God

As a new wind sweeps through the church, passion for God will stir in souls anew. This passion comes as a greater desire to creatively live with Jesus on a daily basis. Rather than observing certain prescribed outward behaviors and rituals, a creative relationship with Jesus takes precedence in spirituality. The inner life becomes one of the soul passionately searching for a deeper relationship with the Divine. Above all else, passion for God becomes the center of everyday life.

In following through with this in a healthy manner, the individual will feel more attuned to fulfilling everyday responsibilities. God-centeredness assists one in fulfilling the tasks of daily life. One who creatively encounters the risen Christ need run no risk of becoming so heavenly that he or she is no earthly good, as long as it is a true relationship with God. A contrived encounter leaves one caught up in an emotional frenzy, feeling inflated and somewhat high-strung, out of touch with daily concerns, personal and communal needs. A genuine meeting with Jesus leaves one's faculties quite alert and able to be applied to tasks at hand in a most expeditious and fruitful manner.

Thus, a passion for God stirs one to forge ahead in life. All activities, whether related to the church or not, are imbued with spiritual life. Nothing fails to be touched by the breath of His spirit. Mature inner development continues as one wholeheartedly lives life with a passionate understanding that God is all and is in all.

Constant Prayer

St. Paul exhorts Christians to pray constantly (Ths 1:5, 17). Constant prayer occurs as the soul remains conscious, ever present with the heart before Jesus. As one goes about daily activities, the heart stays steadfast in God's presence. Throughout the day, one may slip into conscious realizations of Him, but all that is required is the desire to know and live in God.

One abides in constant prayer as he or she feels in touch with their soul. Many have described this as a feeling of centeredness. A holy harmony permeates life and emanates from the core of one's being. Difficulties are approached forthrightly, so resolution and harmony eventually appear. Continual prayer tunes one into continual grace that flows through circumstances and people.

Here I am not stating that continual prayer should create a Pollyanna-ish approach to life. In such a case, one uses prayer as an opiate to dull feelings and blind one to the realities of life. This is a distortion of true prayer and is in fact a characteristic of a very hurting and fear-ridden soul. Genuine continual prayer emboldens one to encounter reality and see it through.

Terror Anticus

The terror anticus is that ancient terror that has so easily taken hold and continues to threaten the most committed of believers. Following the inner way, the inner experience of Jesus, challenges one to ever-deepening growth and consequent dying to egocentricities. This process of letting go, of shedding old patterns of living, can create a certain anxiety within. Since the time of Abraham, men and women have known this terror, especially right before God effects potent healing and change.

Prior to receiving Yahweh's divine word prophesying freedom for the Israelites, the sacred scriptures note, "Now, as the sun was on the point of setting, a trance fell on Abram, and a deep, dark dread descended on him" (Gn 15:12). To stretch himself in faith, meant to feel temporarily terrified. To do what God wanted him to do, Abram faced the terror, as the price to be paid for eventual freedom.

As the new wind of God's spirit blows, temporary anxiety may creep into the steadiest of souls. A new faith experience, letting go of worn out ways, can leave us feeling shaken. In the end, as we endure, a new and fresh freedom in Christ will replace old attitudes worn thin by years of irrelevancy. To cure the anxiety, that ancient anxiety, necessitates nothing short of facing each moment courageously, knowing that Jesus loves you and will see you through and bring to fruition a new passion — a new love for life, for God.

Healing of Soul

This past weekend, the Christian Psychological Foundation hosted, together with the Religious Studies Program at the University of New Mexico, Professor Morton Kelsey to address our conference on Christian spirituality and depth psychology. He spoke on the topic of his then most recent publication, *Psychology, Medicine, and Christian Healing.* After the lectures of the weekend, we concluded with a healing service. Professor Kelsey led a guided prayer in which the hurts of the soul were brought before the healing light and love of Christ.

Throughout the auditorium individuals could be heard gently crying and even sobbing as they felt themselves ushered into the presence of the living Jesus. During this twenty minute prayer, souls were touched and stirred by the love of God. Toward the end, Professor Kelsey encouraged people to pray for people through the laying on of hands. Person after person gently laid their hands on the head of the one next to them and prayed for healing. Healing of mind, body, and spirit was felt that afternoon.

Sometime later, someone approached me and commented, "Professor Kelsey really is in touch with the archetype of the healer." I agreed but thought of it somewhat differently. Professor Kelsey personally knew and was stirred in his soul by the love of God. Consequently, divine compassion and healing flowed both from his teaching and prayer. The passionate love of God always births healing and the cure of souls.

You Are Somebody

To witness the presence of God personally, brings with it an increase in self-esteem. Someone who has touched God feels an appropriate sense of confidence and worth. No longer do belittling feelings and self-criticisms plague such a soul; instead, a new life of energy and self-esteem flows from within.

Quite often in the church I notice low self-esteem masquerading as Christian spirituality. People demean themselves and consider this humility. Nothing could be further from the truth. True humility accords oneself appropriate respect and worth. One suffering from false humility fears accomplishment, outward success, and acclaim. People who receive such merit may be looked down upon and considered egocentric by the one who himself or herself suffers from low self-esteem.

As the spirit of God heals the church, the self-esteem of the individual also will be healed. Christians will manifest this in terms of not only a healthier spirituality, but a creative exchange with the world. Too often Christians have shied away from making political, industrial, financial, or academic contributions to the betterment of mankind for fear that this meant that they were partaking in secular activities. With the new wind blowing, God is seen to be the All in All, the One Who is in all things. Without identifying with the power and egocentricity of the world at large, Christians can make their creative mark in the world. Jesus calls us to be in the world without being of the world.

A healthy sense of self-esteem allows one to live in and contribute to the world without being swept away by its egocentric and narcissistic demands. One's life can remain centered in God while still living and working in the world. An impoverished sense of self-worth causes people to crave power, material gain, and ever widening influence so as to somehow fill up with externals what is missing on the inside. Appropriate self-esteem needs no sort of outward identification since the self is already esteemed and regarded as substantial in its own right.

St. Paul, in his second letter to the Thessalonians, described the manifestations of a healthy self-image as he wrote, "Among the churches of God, we take special pride in you for your perseverance and faith under all the persecutions and hardships you have to bear" (Ths 2:1, 4). Both perseverance and faith characterize a positive self-image. A perseverant soul keeps on living fully and wholeheartedly despite various ordeals. The thought of giving up may prove to be quite tempting at times; however, perseverance bids one to bypass such negativism and continue living life. Armed with the knowledge that God is always at work, the perseverant individual moves through arduous times knowing that God's will can be expected to shine forth soon.

Faith arises from the interior ability to lean on God. When you place your full weight of cares and concerns into His everlasting arms, faith wells up within you. Truly, God's embrace is big enough to handle life's most gargantuan difficulties. With this comes a restful assurance that as we do our best, God's best will definitely come through.

The sense of "being somebody" refers to that very whole and holy feeling that Jesus loves you, is on your side in life, and gifts you with everlasting perseverance and faith. As we all know, without feeling good about ourselves, life seems too overwhelming to bear. Even the slightest of frustrations can threaten to break us down. Fortified with the gospel message that we rest secure in the everlasting arms of Jesus, we are enabled to live life with great confidence and creativity. The new wind of God's spirit blowing through the church will witness the birthing of souls that feel good about themselves, that believe that they are somebody because Jesus loves them. You are somebody because Jesus loves you!

Stand Firm — Stand Strong

> Stand firm, then, Brothers, and keep the traditions that we taught you, whether by word of mouth or by letter. May our Lord, Jesus Christ Himself and God Our Father who has given us His love and, through His grace, such ceaseless encouragement and such sure hope, encourage you and strengthen you in every good word and being. (Ths 2:2, 16–17)

The healing presence of Jesus, coming experientially into one's life, not only improves self-image but imparts a very practical interior attribute of firmness. That is to say, one is more able to stand firm with regard to who he or she is as a person. The unique individuality created by God will not be compromised, but will be lived out with conviction.

The good word and deed St. Paul prays about in these verses refer to those actions and deeds that arise out of one's innermost self, wherein resides the presence of Jesus. All such "center" living is grace filled. Others may not understand this to be so; but, one has the heartfelt sense of being at peace with God as life is lived from this center, one's innermost heart or soul. Typically, a person knows that he or she is living in this centered or balanced manner by the accompanying mental clarity and surety of resolve that coincide with each step taken. A cured soul, one who daily walks the inner way with Jesus, knows this blessed assurance and continues to grow in the knowledge of it.

As I have taught and written about the new wind blowing through the church, much criticism has come my way. I have pondered about the origins of this. For me, criticism that comes from uninformed sources is never easy to take. It feels vicious and quite hurtful.

Often I am tempted to withdraw from saying what I have to say or writing what I feel prompted to write. To stand firm and stand strong is not an easy task for me, especially when insult and degradation come. I literally feel like I am bleeding on the inside when members of my own church, those I have prayed with and embraced, suddenly hurl slanderous charges that, as a depth psychologist, my teachings can in no way be inspired by the Holy Spirit since psychology is of a demonic nature. Of course, I recognize that those who criticize the most do so out of their own inner fear of facing the shadow in their own soul, nonetheless, I can feel the sting of misunderstanding.

On one occasion, in particular, I felt very wobbly. I wrestled with God. Need I preach, teach, and write about the new era of the Holy Spirit? Need I share with others the pearls I have found along the inner way, imparting truths emerging from Christian depth psychology? Wouldn't it be sufficient for me to know and walk along the inner way without writing or teaching?

The Holy Spirit spoke to me, I believe, on these matters. Twice in the early morning His word came. As I uttered the name of Jesus in my morning hour of prayer, I saw with the eyes of my soul three words: "Freud touched God." Coming to my senses, I felt rejuvenated with greater mental clarity and personal assurance than I had known for a long time. The tradition of depth psychology pioneered by Freud and Jung I now knew to be Holy Spirit–inspired and to be brought into the service of the gospel.

Not too long after this, the Holy Spirit spoke deeply to me again during my early morning prayer. I heard the words, "You must pour yourself out, and pour yourself out, and pour yourself out for my people." As I ended my prayer, a new grace to stand firm, to stand strong filled me. To proclaim the good news of the "Deep Gospel" is God's will for my life. As a new wind blows through His church, souls will feel the inspiration to seek Him and to seek Him deeply.

I pray that you and I together may feel the inspiration to seek Him more and more deeply each day. Let your heart stand firm as you seek Him within your soul. Know that he will speak to you in moments of prayerful inspiration, through the perception of his voiceless voice, in dreams and visions, and in the words of those who love and care for you. He will speak and guide you through the sacred scriptures as you feel a new and more fervent desire to read and understand them. The fresh breath of the Holy Spirit brings all that is in darkness to light, heals unresolved pains and fears, and unleashes creative energies untold.

And now, in the words of St. Paul, "May the Lord of Peace himself give you peace at all times and in every way" (Ths 2:3, 16).

Church of Anxiety — Church of Awe

As the new wind of the Holy Spirit blows we will witness a time of increasing anxiety in the church. Everyone has believed that everything would continue as it has been for decades, indeed centuries. No longer will everything remain the same. As changes increase, anxiety builds. Only for those who have eyes to see and ears to hear will anxiety be heeded as the presence of God's transforming power. With an open heart, a heart yielded to truth, anxiety can be transformed into awe.

A great Christian depth psychologist once noted that anxiety accompanies the beginnings of conversion. Old egocentric patterns of living that one has grown comfortable with, begin to crumble and the soul is left unsteady. With the familiar passing away, insecurities abound. Anxiety results whenever we attempt to hold on to old forms that need to pass away. A call to conversion beckons us forth to the anxiety and into transformation and greater sanctity. As the church, those gathered together by a commonality of spirit, faces and deals with its anxiety, new life will flourish.

Without everything continuing to be as it always has been, people are left with no choice but to seek God for themselves. When the individual no longer completely depends upon a god-like institution that proclaims rules and regulations regarding every aspect of life, then a more personal faith must be established. What was once external must now be internal. An intimate relationship with the Risen Christ must now replace an immature dependency upon external authority. Those who refuse this call to inner change will feel crippled by a tormenting anxiety. They will, perhaps, become extremely rigid and narrow-minded in matters of faith. This enables them to feel an elusive certitude that God's workings have not changed and that everything is as it always has been. In the end, this will be known for what it is — a mere strengthening of egocentric defenses that alleviates anxiety for the moment and exacerbates it eventually.

Thus, interior anxiety signals the voice of the Master calling us to greater inner healing. Once through the anxiety, awe gradually permeates the soul. Awe is the transcendent perception of God's presence anew filled with wonder, delight, and mystery. As the storm of anxiety passes, an awesome and new beauty of the Divine surfaces. Never before has God seemed so magnificent, rich, and deep. He is truly experienced as the All in All, the One Who holds all things together, the Magnificent Lover.

Beware

The dire importance of Jesus and Jesus alone in spirituality is brought home through the following anecdote: One Sunday morning, the parish pastor announced that Jesus Christ would be present for the 10:30 a.m. Mass on the following Sunday. As expected, people crowded into the church to see Him. At the end of Mass everyone came up to Him, shook His hand, and some even invited Him for dinner and to accept lodging in their home. Jesus thanked them for their invitations but He had already decided to spend the rest of the day and on into the night in the church. All the people understood.

Early Monday morning, Jesus slipped out of the church before any-one had arrived for early morning Mass. Once the priest and the people came for Mass, they found the word "BEWARE." All over the church was scribbled "BEWARE." On the front of the pulpit, on the back and front doors, on the stained glass windows, on the altar, and even on the Bible was scribbled "BEWARE." Throughout the church, written in different colors of ink and paint, were the words "BEWARE, BEWARE, BEWARE..."

At first the people were outraged, shocked, horrified. They wanted to clean up their church and wipe away any trace of this sacrilegious con-duct. Only the thought that Jesus Himself had written these words restrained them.

Slowly the meaning of the word "BEWARE" began to stir in their souls. Now each time the Bible was opened to the reading of the scriptures, they saw the word, "BEWARE." When they heard the scriptures, they were now able to learn from them without trying to box God in. As they were more willing to beware of the sacraments, they experienced a new grace in their souls and old superstitions fell away. The priest began to beware of his power and authority so that he was now more able to help them without exercising undue control and domination. People began to beware of prayer so that they could still converse with God without losing their own sense of responsible action.

Now, as the story goes, these parishioners have the shocking word "BEWARE" emblazoned in neon lights at the front of their church so that all who pass by, even in the dark of night, would be able to wonder about the mysterious word of Jesus: "BEWARE."

Anxiety into Awe

St. Paul prays, "And may He so confirm your hearts in holiness that you may be blameless in the sight of our God and Father when our Lord Jesus comes with all His holy ones" (1 Ths 3:13). Confirming one's heart in holiness means that all manner of blame and unconsciousness is being uprooted from the soul. As the soul sees what it needs to see, anxiety subsides and gives way to awe. As one sees God more clearly, wonder and awe overcome the soul.

The coming of our Lord Jesus with all His holy ones occurs whenever the soul encounters God anew. As the church knows a fresh outpouring of the Holy Spirit, then the true participation of all believers in the Mystical Body of Christ will become more and more a reality. The saints still on earth together with the saints who have passed into heaven form the company of holy ones always abiding in the presence of Jesus. Truly, then we begin to live a church that is awesome.

Many who work for the church feel nothing but strain and anxiety. Innumerable times I have heard, "If you really want to lose your faith, just work for the church a while." Unfortunately, there can be some truth in this assertion. Anxiety has plagued the workings of the church. An institution that attempts to enforce a compendium of strict rules and regulations, of ways of doing things and not doing things, becomes anxiety-ridden and tormented. Those who work in such a situation feel the effects in their soul. They feel depleted, sapped of vital faith, and burned out on the church.

In contrast to this, when believers work together out of a shared inner experience of Jesus, vitality abounds. A mutual love of God and a growing daily knowledge of Him supports and encourages personal faith. A sense of awe accompanies daily life in the place of a bedraggled and anxiety-ridden existence. God is a god of awe and all who come to know Him in this time of a new wind blowing, will share experientially in the mystery of His awesome presence.

The Inner Way of Transformation

Holy men and women down through the ages have noted three phases of spiritual development and transformation. Since we are addressing psychological phenomenology, we will use a different language, a psychological rather than a theological one, to describe this process. First of all, there is the experience of crisis or purgation; secondly, one comes into the knowledge of the tremendum — the dark side of God; thirdly, divine illumination floods the soul as the inner way is experienced as a personal reality.

The phase of purgation or crisis is one in which the individual feels an assault on all that has been held near and dear. Former ways of living, relating to others, and perceiving one's relationship to God are turned upside down and inside out. Usually a crisis of some sort precipitates all of this. When we have placed too much emphasis on one aspect of life, typically a more external and superficial way of relating to life, a crisis comes in order to purge us of this imbalance. It may come in the form of a marital or familial crisis, financial difficulties, conflict within the church or a personal sense of increasing meaninglessness in life. As one is willing to walk through this crisis and learn what must be learned, the second phase of development is gradually entered into.

Experiencing the tremendum, the dark side of God, is a much neglected reality in the life of many Christians. We prefer to characterize God in an overly light fashion. We consider Him to be sweet and nice, meek and gentle, ever patient and enduring. In truth, God can be quite demanding and stern, calling us to Himself, to our own Center without compromise. God is unwilling to tolerate anything that would separate us from Him and would obliterate all that interferes with the creative life. This is the dark side of God. Our choice is to resist it or to flow with this dark and mysterious grace. With resistance, anxiety and torment abound. As the soul cooperates with the Divine in this matter, transformation and illumination ensue.

Having known the dark side of God, the soul gradually moves into a state of greater illumination in which the kingdom of heaven is now personally understood to be an inner kingdom, an inner way of knowing Jesus. Outer development and changes, actions to improve the lot of humankind, flow from this interior grace. Without it, the best intentions and social actions eventually are blown away as chaff. Inspiration that results from inner illumination creates sound enterprises and ministries. Thus, spiritual illumination bestows a balanced knowledge of God as the Tremendous Lover with both a light side and dark side — the dark side obliterating all that interferes with His creative love and the light side that bestows everlasting love.

Ruth, a sixty-five-year-old ardent church secretary, recounted her experience of the dark side of God.

For years I had been working twelve even fourteen hours a day at the church. Soon I was working so much that I had no time alone, no time to be alone with God. I became increasingly stressed and anxious. My back began to give me problems. The pain became so excruciating that I sought the consultation of an orthopedic surgeon.

The only thing the doctor could do was pump me more and more full of medication. I felt no significant relief. Finally, I decided simply to ask God what the problem was. One afternoon, after having received communion, I spent some time quietly alone in the church. As clear as could be the definite thought came to me, "I will no longer support you in your overwork, I want you to be with Me, to have more time for Me." That was all it took, I understood.

Now I work only four hours a day at the church. Whatever I can't do, God will have to bring someone else along to take care of it. Within twenty-four hours of realizing that overwork was the cause of my back problems, I felt completely healed. Since that time, now one year ago, I had never had a minute's problem with my back. God wanted me to give up the overwork that was interfering with my relationship with Him. Once I understood what God wanted me to understand, I was healed.

To See Jesus in All Things

As the soul becomes oriented more and more to the Center within, so Jesus is seen more and more in all things. The hand of God works in and through each circumstance, each turn of events, every mundane task, and even through extraordinary happenings. No longer at odds with herself, the soul feels at one, at peace, and so true reality dawns upon her — the reality that in Him, in Jesus, all things hold together.

The process involved in the healing of toxicity demands constant vigilance, wakefulness. As one's eyes are opened, so the soul awakens to the reality of the living Christ within. Ever so deliberately, healing flows from the deep well of the Holy Spirit. In the midst of cure — the process of cure — the person lives with greater centeredness and peace. Truly, he or she feels born anew, as though a new wind has blown through life, effecting deep and lasting transformation. From death to life the soul has come.

In knowing deep cure, many state that they feel themselves to be alive for the first time. Their five senses take on a new luster. One person explained:

> The smells that I smell seem so new. The colors that have always been around me in the world, now look brighter and more vivid. The food that I thought that I always enjoyed, I now savor. My ears delight to hear classical music and heartfelt conversation. Even the air feels so crisp on my skin. I feel alive.

To be alive enough to see Jesus in all things means having eyes for the supernatural. A pathologically disturbed personality hallucinates and lives in a world of delusion. However, a soul on the path of integration and healing often discovers a mysterious and supernatural world that gradually reveals itself. Depth psychology has referred to it as the collective unconscious. Happenings that transcend empiricism and the logical order of things can take place. The soul on the inner way knows and feels both the natural and the supernatural worlds.

St. Paul describes an anticipated supernatural happening as he prophesies the Second Coming of Christ:

> At the signal given by the voice of the Archangel and the trumpet of God, the Lord Himself will come down from Heaven, those who have died in Christ will be the first to rise, and only after that shall we who remain alive be taken up in the clouds, together with them to meet the Lord in the air. This is the way we shall be with the Lord forever. (1 Ths 4:16–17)

Since the supernatural realm is seen only by those with eyes to see and heard only by those with ears to hear, it can be surmised that those who recognize Jesus in all things in their daily life, will see Him in His Second Coming. Just as many miss the reality of the spiritual world that is manifest each night in dreams, so a major supernatural occurrence such as the Second Coming will be overlooked, perhaps not even perceived by a vast majority.

I have been asked whether I believe in the literal Second Coming. In other words, do I actually think that Jesus Himself will return with the drama depicted by St. Paul in his letters to the Thessalonians. Will the Archangel blow a trumpet signaling His return, loud enough for all who have ears to hear? Will Jesus come down from Heaven visibly enough to be seen by all who have eyes to see? Will believers, all those who know firsthand the reality of the inner experience of Jesus, be taken up in the clouds to meet the Lord in the air and so remain with the Lord forever? Do I believe all of this?

I do believe in the literal Second Coming of Jesus with all the drama and mystery conveyed by Paul to the church in Thessalonia. Psychologically, I would describe it as an encounter with the archetype of the miracle. A supernatural occurrence takes place in time and space of such proportions as to affect great numbers of people at once. Biblical precedent confirms the possibility of such an event. Enoch was taken up to Heaven without having to experience physical death. The prophet Elijah was carried to the heavenlies in a fiery chariot also without having to undergo the normal process of dying. At the time of His Ascension, the scriptures record that Jesus appeared in the same manner to hundreds of people at once. A supernatural happening such as the Second Coming seems quite plausible to me both on the grounds of biblical precedent and sound psychological thought.

Of primary concern, however, is St. Paul's emphasis on being with the Lord forever. As healing of the soul occurs, the sense of being with God develops more and more interiorly. Throughout the course of life, an awareness of God, in the midst of daily life, takes hold of the soul. An event such as the Second Coming would in no way overwhelm, or perhaps even surprise, one walking along the inner way. It would be an outward sign of an ongoing internal reality.

At the beginning of her psychotherapy, Rachel spoke of the following vision: "During my normal time of prayer, all of a sudden, right before me, I saw the crucified Christ. I heard the words, 'Come, follow me.' This vision passed within seconds."

As we explored the meaning of this vision, Rachel felt it to be a supernatural occurrence in that it profoundly moved her soul and enabled her to peer into a realm that was normally unavailable to her. As the result of this vision, she more earnestly committed herself to the process of psychotherapy, which she now understood to be God's call to her. Through psychotherapy she could experience a dying to her old ego-centric ways. The inner journey called her to follow Christ in a more in-depth manner. This supernatural happening inspired her to more honestly and forthrightly deal with deeper emotions and therein encounter Jesus.

Rachel was not prone toward psychoses. That is to say, her psychological structure had never been weakened sufficiently to cause her to lose contact with reality and hear voices or see visions of a condemning and pathological nature. The pain in her everyday life brought her into psychotherapy, but she was in no way a candidate for hospitalization or medication. In other words, Rachel was quite a "normal" person. The supernatural broke in on her consciousness when she least expected it and imparted grace.

Authentic supernatural experiences with Jesus can be discerned by their impulse toward health. Such manifestations enable people to live a more creative and loving life. Seemingly supernatural occurrences that leave the person feeling fractured, out of sorts with the self and others need to be questioned with regard to their validity. They may in all probability be from a pathological or demonic source. In such cases, it is highly recommended that the person immediately seek professional counsel.

Thus, to see Jesus in all things permits the individual to maintain a creative exchange with the unconscious both on the personal and collective level. Such a one freely deals with his or her emotional life in a way that self-understanding and growth and interpersonal relationships continue. Together with this, a sense of being at home in the collective unconscious, the spiritual world, also develops. Since the kingdom of heaven is very much a "now" reality it makes sense that one living in the kingdom maintains a healthy exchange with both the natural and supernatural worlds. In so doing, the personality matures in a healthy and creative fashion.

The cure of toxicity thus demands that one gradually sees Jesus more and more in all things. The process of healing is quite unrelenting and is never satisfied until the ego yields itself to constant change and development. Rather than gauging oneself according to narrow doctrinal confines, whether of a religious or psychological nature, the creative way alerts one to the necessity of following Jesus and Jesus alone. Anxiety after anxiety, misery after misery, futility after futility will be known by one who counters this heavenly pursuit by rigid refusal of increased consciousness. To adamantly oppose the light of Christ entails suffering enormous neurotic, and perhaps even psychotic, misery. The healing way is the way of following Jesus alone.

The way of Jesus is the way of self-reflection, painstaking truthfulness, and a commitment to seek and find interior fulfillment and wholeness. Even though one may not espouse a formal religious commitment to the Risen Christ, still the inner way may be followed. Those who live a life of creativity that benefits both self and humankind, live a life in Jesus. Consciously they may disavow any connection with Christianity or Jesus; unconsciously, however, they move according to the spirit of Him who knows no bigoted limits of love. All that matters for salvation is that one abide in Jesus.

The mysterious transformation that affects the soul abiding in Jesus is detailed by St. Simeon, the New Theologian:

> But, O, what intoxication of light,
> O what movements of fire!
> O what swirlings of the flame in me,
> Miserable one that I am, coming from you and your glory!
> The glory I know it and I say it is your Holy Spirit,
> who has the same nature with you and the same honor, O Word;
> He is the same rays of the same glory,
> of the same essence, he alone with your Father
> and with you, O Christ, O God of the universe!
> I fall in adoration before You.
> I thank You that You, even when I was sitting in darkness
> revealed Yourself to me, You enlightened me,
> You granted me to see the light of Your countenance
> that is unbearable to all.
> I remain seated in the middle of the darkness, I know,
> but, while I was there surrounded by darkness,
> You appeared as light, illuminating me,
> completely from your total light.
> And I became light in the night,
> I was found in the midst of darkness.
> Neither the darkness extinguished Your light completely, nor
> did the light dissipate the visible darkness,

that they were together, yet completely separate,
without confusion, far from each other,
surely not at all mixed,
except in the same spot where they filled everything,
so it seems to me.
So I am in the light, yet I am found in the middle of the darkness.
So I am in the darkness yet still I am in the middle of the light.

Five

Healing the Family Curse

The curse. Sound a little scary? It is scary; indeed it is terrifying. Dark and destructive human feelings can be consciously or unconsciously projected into another person: a curse has been imparted. One who is vulnerable to the effects of a curse, which is toxic by nature, can suffer quite miserably.

Thus, a curse is the projection of destructive feelings, involving both emotional and spiritual energy, into another human being. In such cases, one experiences a pressure, a compulsion, a pressing expectation to act in a particular manner, to live in a predetermined way. When projections are directed into a person, one has been injected with toxic emotional and spiritual energies such as rage, despair, and confusion. A projection into an individual is typically unconscious and quite debilitating.

The family sets the scene for the enactment of curses. In order for a curse to take effect, openness, vulnerability, and proximity in time and space must be present. Thus, family members maintain key positions to inflict curses into each other. They come in the form of demanding expectations, mixed messages, overt or covert desires for revenge and the demise of another, and subtle coercions that are bent on exercising manipulation and domination over another. The curse can be alive and well in families, whether it is acknowledged or not.

"A father's blessing makes his children's house firm, while a mother's curse tears up its foundations" (Eccl. 3:9). Parents can, consciously or unconsciously, lay curses upon their children. A parent may not realize it, but his or her attitudes or actions that foster dependency, immaturity, misunderstanding, and thwarted growth in a child, constitute curses. Children need blessings, not curses, to thrive and develop.

> How blessed is anyone who fears Yahweh, who delights in His commandments! His descendants shall be powerful on earth, the race of the honest shall receive blessings: riches and wealth for his family; his uprightness stands forever. (Ps 112:1–3)

Blessings, directed from the parents to the children, solidify the family and each individual within the family. Individual interior growth brings forth external blessings within relationships and family life. Blessings, rather than cursings, are imparted, individual to individual. Each person's creativity as a unique and worthy soul is supported and cultivated. In a healthy family in which blessings rather than cursings abound, the family serves to support and nourish the individual; in an unhealthy family, the individual is dominated by the family and is expected to serve the needs of the family without regard for him or her as an independent person of worth and value. Blessings in the context of a family enable one to explore his or her unique talents, interests, and ways of relating to and with life. Cultivating an appropriate independence for individuals within the family actually acts to create a very freeing and substantive intimacy. Without the constraints of unhealthy ties, feeling possessed by the family as a whole, the individual freely chooses to partake of family life and may, ideally, discover great joy and fulfillment in family relationships.

At least four different curses plague the family: (1) "Don't feel"; (2) "Don't trust"; (3) "Don't talk"; (4) "Don't grow." Each curse potentially constellates a disease complex such as alcoholism and various minor addictions, drug and sexual/relational compulsions, addiction to rage, and chronic physical ailments. Together with this, a messiah/martyr complex is also needed in order to sustain the power of the curse. In other words, each curse may manifest a particular disease complex that is enabled by at least one other individual, referred to as the messiah/martyr, in the life of the afflicted soul.

The "Don't Feel" Curse

"Blessed be the God and Father of our Lord Jesus Christ, who has blessed us with all the spiritual blessings of heaven and Christ" (Eph 1:3). All spiritual blessings necessary to know salvation and fullness of life in this world and the next have been bequeathed to the believer. All manner of experiencing God, including the full range of emotional experience and expression, are included in spiritual blessings. To feel fully, permits one to know fully, firsthand, the Risen Jesus. He then encourages a gradual unfolding of the Father's plan for one's life.

I remember both hearing and seeing the dramatic display of rage given by Father Patrick in the emergency room of a local hospital. Having been called in by Father Patrick's superior to provide psychological consultation, I attempted to understand the source of Father Patrick's emotional chaos. One hour earlier, he had attempted suicide by ingesting barbiturates and alcohol. He yelled out at me, "No one understood how awful I have felt. My whole community told me that I would be alright. 'Don't worry about it, you'll be alright.' That's all that I've heard. Nobody will listen to me. I hope they can hear me now."

The "don't feel" curse frequently comes through spoken messages such as "You'll be alright," "Don't worry about it," "Don't feel bad," "You're just too sensitive." These statements urge one to suppress powerful feelings that need to be understood.

For too long, Father Patrick had been told by his religious community and by his family of origin not to feel. Drinking more and more alcohol enabled him to numb his emotional pain. Alcoholism became the means by which he lived out the "don't feel" curse that had been inflicted into him. Despite the supposedly biological and genetic tendencies toward alcohol, the "don't feel" curse plays an unmistakably overpowering role within the life of an alcoholic.

The "don't feel" curse may also give rise to other more minor addictions such as the incessant watching of television, compulsive housekeeping, and even gossip. Emotions are lulled to sleep by watching television program after television program. Likewise, a person who feels distraught on the inside can be tempted to meticulously and compulsively do housework such as vacuuming, dusting and cleaning out cupboards. They expend so much energy on the outside that they never have to face their feelings on the inside. In a like manner, gossip provides a release of emotional energy by constantly talking in a denigrating manner about other people. With a tongue aching to chatter and ears itching to hear, the gossip tears down others and finds a destructive channel for the release of what is often a torrent of unrelenting resentment and rage that has never been felt or faced.

As the curse gives way to blessing, God's will gradually unfolds. "He has let us know the mystery of His purpose, according to His good pleasure which He determined beforehand in Christ" (Eph 1:9). The healthy family guides the individual in discovering the mystery of God's will in his or her life. This blessing assists one to follow God rather than following the dictates of a possessive and entangled family system.

Many months after our first meeting, Father Patrick confided:

> I never wanted to be a priest. I wanted to be a simple religious brother. My mother told me that I had to become a priest for the sake of my family. A family with a priest in it was a holy family and was assured of heaven. In many ways, I was sacrificed by my

mother for the sake of getting my whole family into heaven. It's absurd, of course, but this is the way my family thought.

Three days before my ordination, I told my superiors that I doubted whether I should be ordained. I really felt that I wanted to remain a brother. They dismissed my feelings, as did my mother, but for a different, although very similar reason. The Order needed priests and all aspirants prior to their ordination naturally suffered doubts, I was told. My superiors informed me that this was one last temptation, prompted by the devil, to turn me away from my heavenly call. Once again, I was sacrificed, this time for the sake of the Order.

After ordination, I became increasingly miserable. My feelings, indeed my soul, had been violated by my mother, my family, and my religious community. I did not have the strength to go my own way. Drinking helped me to block out my pain and go on living a life that was pleasing to everyone else but me.

To not feel means to lose contact with God's presence within and the ever-unfolding mystery of His divine plan at work in one's life. Those under such a curse inevitably suffer a sickness of one sort or another. Alcoholism is a common ailment of soul and body that arises from the "don't feel" curse. Life is meant to be lived purposely and meaningfully with depth of feeling.

"And it is in Him that we have received our heritage, marked out beforehand as we were, under the plan of the One who guides all things as He decides by His own will, chosen to be, for the praise of His glory" (Eph 1:11). God has marked out beforehand the course one is to take in life. Following this inner way brings with it a greater interior satisfaction and outer accomplishment. Things seem to fall into place and one is permitted to fully live up to his or her potential as long as the life calling is observed.

With the "don't feel" curse, that which was instituted in the soul before birth is thwarted, suppressed. Rather than fullness of life, a person grinds through daily existence. Feeling has been lost and, therefore, there is no intuition regarding God's plan for one's life. A sense of mission and destiny has been abandoned. In such a state, one feels like a lost soul.

Only by facing the truth of emotional feeling and spiritual longing does one's destiny become clear. Blessing obliterates cursing through intense and painstaking soul-searching in which God is encountered as a living reality within the soul. Freedom from the "don't feel" curse hinges on darkness being brought to light, feelings surfacing from the depths, the cross leading to the crown.

Some years after Father Patrick and I had completed successful, long-term treatment in psychotherapy, I received another call from his religious superior. Before answering the telephone in my office, I was informed by my secretary that the superior wished to consult with me on my availability to assist the Order in determining suitable candidates for the priesthood; but, before I was to talk to the superior, another priest wished to speak with me for a moment. On the other end of the line, I heard, "Dr. DeBlassie, this is Brother Patrick." I recognized the voice, but I couldn't place the name with the face.

I'm sure you remember me. I am Father Patrick, at least to the majority of people. After our work was completed together, I decided to begin referring to myself simply as Brother Patrick, especially when introducing myself to new friends. I did not feel it was misleading since, in the rule of our order, we are first to be brothers one to another and priesthood is of secondary importance. Thanks to our work, I feel free. Others might want me to be their Father Patrick, but on the inside, I am, and always will be, Brother Patrick now. I have found myself. All has gone well through the years since I have seen you. I am free now, free to be fully me.

Father Patrick had been transformed into Brother Patrick and knew the freedom of living out God's plan for his life. With the blessing of feeling fully, he knew who he was as a person, as an individual created in God's image and likeness. The toxic family curse had been lifted. God's blessing, determined beforehand in Christ, flowed freely and fully in his life.

Healing the Messiah/Martyr Complex

The ongoing nature of a family curse almost always involves the active participation of a messiah/martyr. This person serves to enable the one who has been cursed, so to speak, to continue on in his or her misery. The alcoholic usually has the assistance of one who acts as the martyr and puts up with the life abuse inflicted by the alcoholic. The gossip always has a person, or persons, who will listen to defaming talk. The workaholic inflicts emotional pain on his or her spouse and other close family members as long as such compulsiveness is tolerated.

The messiah believes that he or she is meant to help the sufferer no matter the personal cost. In fact, the more the messiah suffers, and thus becomes a martyr, the more he or she believes that they are actually fulfilling God's will for their life. The messiah/martyr complex is confused with authentic love. A complex-ridden person of this sort colludes with the misery of another and in no way assists in understanding and working it through.

The messiah/martyr takes on responsibility for everyone's problems. The subtle belief is, "If I don't do it, it won't get done." Responsibility, obligation, and guilt characterize the messiah. If someone is not helped, guilt readily attacks the conscience. A burdensome obligation to relieve human suffering plagues the messiah. Without a doubt, the messiah soon becomes the martyr who complains of suffering even more than the afflicted one does.

Love or Blame

The messiah/martyr confuses love and the toxic complex that causes interminable sick suffering, ostensibly for the sake of others. Love supports and assists others in taking responsibility for their own life. One possessed by the messiah/martyr complex constantly attempts to take the responsibility of living for other people. Rather than encouraging others toward strength and independence, the martyr instead unconsciously fosters dependence and emotional immaturity.

Messiahs hide away from facing the truth about others by claiming that they do not want to blame anyone. In so doing, they rob others of the freedom that can result from taking responsibility for one's own life. Blaming has no place in the context of real growth and development. Truth-facing, on the other hand, is a necessity for spiritual and emotional progress. By constantly facing the truth regarding ourselves and others, we see other people for what they are, not for what we want them to be. No blame is levied here.

Thus, for the messiah, facing the truth of his or her need to assume responsibility for the total welfare of others lest guilt should be incurred, is the first step toward freedom. Certain family members may desire, indeed demand, that they be partially or completely cared for as though they were helpless victims in life. The messiah need not blame them for their egocentricities. All that is necessary is that the messiah begin the process of realizing that one's personal life is all that can be effectively lived. No person can take responsibility for another person. Each man, each woman, must make the decision in his or her own time to live his or her own life.

Helping the Help-aholic

Sharon sat in front of me and sobbed, "I've always felt like I have to help him, but I can't do it anymore. The more I try and help him, the more hurt I feel. He's not even trying to help himself anymore. Everything has been resting on my shoulders and I have had enough of that."

After twenty years of marriage, Sharon decided to seek help because she needed to help others, especially her husband, so badly that it actually hurt her. His alcoholism had been devastating the family for years on end. She had made excuse after excuse for him. She told her children that he didn't mean to do what he did, that one of these days, he would just get over it. Twenty years of excuse-making had finally caught up with her. It left her feeling discouraged, depressed, and burned out.

Unfortunately, it took this crisis before she was ready to consider letting go of taking responsibility for her husband's life. She could not "get better" for him. She could not find happiness for him. She could not change him.

During our next session, we both confronted him. She stated, "You need to enter an alcoholism treatment program and get involved in AA or else I'm leaving you. I have the name of an attorney who will help me begin the process of separation. I've had it. You either do something to pull your life together or I'm gone."

Enraged, he bolted out of my office. We thought it best to begin proceedings for separation. Little did we know that that very evening he would admit himself, voluntarily, to a local alcoholism treatment program. Many months later, he humbly admitted, "You really shook me up when you drew the line like that. I never thought you had it in you. I thought you would take whatever I dished out. Well, I'm here to tell you now that you are not responsible for my sobriety. I am responsible for my sobriety."

Twenty years of marital pain had finally been transformed into a mutual desire for growth and well-being. She gradually resumed responsibility for her life and only her life. She offered others loving encouragement, support, and her prayers, but she could not assume responsibility for their well-being. Sharon, to this very day, is a recovering help-aholic.

The "Don't Trust" Curse

The second toxic curse we will examine is the "don't trust" curse. Parents inflict this curse on children as they breathe attitudes of fearfulness and mistrust towards others, toward God, and toward their very selves. Children learn that those outside the family cannot really be trusted as honest and genuine people. God is viewed as "out to get you." Personal feelings, intuitions, and aspirations are rejected whenever they conflict with the family ideal. The family and the family alone is to be "trusted."

Of course, even family members are not actually trusted. Children may comply with parental demands but, in their innermost selves, they despise this domination and perceive their parents as cold and ruthless. It is not that children trust their parents, rather, they are overcome by the force of parental authority to submit. Understanding and communication have been completely violated in the family afflicted by the "don't trust" curse and, in their place, reign control and harsh authoritarianism.

Parents can afflict children with toxic mistrust. Religious superiors may choose to use their power to grind down the will of those in their charge, turning men into boys and women into girls. Prayer group leaders may assume the guise of inflated self-importance that acts to intimidate others and bring them under the sway of a manipulative charisma. In all, inflicting the "don't trust" curse thwarts human growth, development, and independence, and is therefore a curse.

The manifestation of the curse frequently involves addictive symptoms such as drug abuse, sexual compulsions and even religious fanaticism. As people learn not to trust other people, their own inner feelings, or the providence of God, other solutions are sought. Mind-altering chemicals, various sexual experiences, or compulsive religious observances, all act to suppress and deny interior fearfulness. Such a one feels all alone in a hostile and cruel world. Under the burden of the "don't trust" curse, men and women crumble spiritually and emotionally.

Grace in Your Life

"Because it is by grace that you have been saved, through faith; not by anything of your own, but by a gift from God; not by anything that you have done, so that nobody can claim the credit" (Eph 2:8). The grace of life surrounds us. Not as anything that we have earned, but as a free gift. We can potentially know grace flowing through and through every moment of life. To know grace means to know a quality of interior certitude that God always guides and provides. Trusting in Him is the walk of faith that increases the flow of grace and the awareness of that grace.

Trusting in the Divine gradually frees one from the "don't trust" curse. Those addicted to drugs, sexual acting-out, and compulsive external observances of religion, discover freedom only by encountering the Holy within. Grace saves the soul in that it liberates one from the tyranny of compulsions that arise out of deep fear and mistrust. Addictive behaviors attempt to bind up inner anxieties and terrors; however, in reality, they only lead to emptiness and never to fullness of life. They leave one high and dry. Only grace, making itself felt through faith, frees the hurting soul.

The psyche, crippled by mistrust, sees the world, people, and God as hostile and angry. This has less to do with reality and more to do with unresolved intra-psychic rage. What has not been dealt with on the inside is projected to the outside. In actuality, such individuals are tormented by their own rage toward those who have hurt them. Rather than admitting this guilt-laden horror, they repress their feelings and project them onto outer events or people. Everyone is angry, seemingly, with the person who himself or herself is packed with resentment, bitterness, and fury.

Only the knowledge of a loving Savior breaks this curse. On the shores of the Lake of Galilee, Jesus ministered to the lame, the crippled, the blind, and the dumb. With hardly a word being spoken, they sat down at his feet, completely assured of His safe love. He would not hurt them as others had hurt them. The mistrust that had, perhaps, symbolically manifested itself in physical symptoms, melted away in the presence of the Man from Galilee. "The crowds were astonished to see the dumb speaking, the cripple whole again, the lame walking, and the blind with their sight, and they praised the God of Israel" (Mt 15:31).

Grace in Your Soul

As one is aligned with the flow of grace in life through outer situations and events, the awareness of inner grace, grace abiding in the soul, gradually emerges. One knows a sense of homecoming, a feeling of returning to the heart of the Self. No longer feeling cut off and internally dismembered, the individual recognizes that all life flows from within. Feelings and other inner voices are heeded and respected as contributing to continued growth. Grace issues forth from all genuine interior promptings and insights.

St. Paul, in his letter to the Ephesians, describes the wondrous reception of the integration and peace with the Self that follows a grace-filled conversion: "So you are no longer aliens or foreign visitors; you are fellow-citizens with the holy people of God and part of God's household. You are built upon the foundations of the apostles and prophets, and Christ Jesus himself is the cornerstone. Every structure knit together in Him grows into a holy temple in the Lord; and you too, in Him, are being built up into a dwelling-place of God in the Spirit" (Eph 2:19–22).

The alienation from the Self, indeed, from the presence of Jesus dwelling within, no longer plagues one who abides with the continual awareness of grace. The "don't trust" curse obviously dissipates as grace in the soul bountifully increases. At one with God and the self, an individual grows in trust and well-being. Rather than relying on ingesting mind-altering drugs, or partaking in irresponsible sexual activities, one's relationship with Christ Jesus in the soul provides sustenance and nourishment beyond what one could ever ask or imagine. Superfluous, and heretofore compulsive and toxic religious practices, give way to the inner experience of Christ Jesus — the One Who resides in the Holy of Holies and desires all to come into a loving communion with Him.

"Does anybody want me?" asked a very forlorn-looking woman. Her parents had been addicted to cocaine. She had been involved in a highly promiscuous lifestyle in an effort to find interior wholeness and someone to care for her. By the time she was twelve years of age, she had been cared for by seven or eight different relatives. After the death of her parents, it seems as though no one wanted to care for her. She grew up wondering, "Does anybody want me?"

Intensive long-term psychotherapy enabled her to experience a spiritual conversion that witnessed a very remarkable transformation in her life. In her words, "I really never believed anyone wanted me. Now I feel God on the inside of me. The more I get to know myself, the more I feel that I know and trust Him. I've come home now. I have found what I have been looking for."

The "People Pleasing" Curse

Following on the heels of the "don't trust" curse is the concomitant expression of the people-pleasing mentality, in itself, a debilitating toxin. Those addicted to drugs, sexual indulgences, and religious compulsions are often linked together with another person who can be described as a people-pleaser. A type of messiah or martyr, the people-pleaser enables the addictive curse to be maintained. He or she puts up with anything and everything so long as others like him or her. A people-pleaser is willing to sacrifice emotional and spiritual health and well-being for the sake of being pleasing to others.

In church circles, unhealthy religiosity demands conformity. Anyone who steps out of line, who does not please the group, is ostracized. Independent thought or inspiration is downplayed in the face of collective rulings. Groups of church people entangle one another in possessive and oppressive ways of relating to each other and God. Everyone wants to please everyone else. The church then becomes a neurotic unit composed of people-pleasing people.

The danger in all of this is that no one is able to take a critical stance. Everyone agrees with everyone else, no one sees or articulates truth, everyone is on the bandwagon talking about God in the same way and going nowhere. When a mob is the object of faith rather than the indwelling presence of the Holy Spirit, spirituality deteriorates into nothing more than an experience of spirits such as control, domination, and manipulation. Mob psychology, not the inspiration of the Holy Ghost, fuels the fire of this type of ostensibly religious fervor.

Without trusting in the Self, the image of God within each human soul, people get tangled up in people. Personal boundaries and limits are obliterated in order to maintain unhealthy ties to the group. The Self is lost as the people-pleasing pressure dominates the personality. In a very real sense, one has lost touch with his or her soul whenever people-pleasing is a prime motivator. Only through the conscious awareness of this particular messiah/martyr complex and the deliberate decision to engage in in-depth psychotherapy that leads one into an encounter with God, will individual or familial healing occur.

Believe in Yourself

Believing in yourself is a central element in the Christian message. "In Him, we are bold enough to approach God in complete confidence, through our faith in Him" (Eph 3:12). Approaching God with confidence requires a sense of personal worth, seeing oneself as loved by God. Such a person trusts his or her innermost feelings and perceptions: trust is his or her relationship with God.

The sufferer of a messiah/martyr complex arising out of the "don't trust" curse, has lost the sense of believing in the self. Others are relied upon for affirmation, direction, and approval. An internal realization of personal integrity seems non-existent to such people. The greatest miracle of all — belief in the self — has been thwarted.

I remember a number of ministers confronting me on the validity of believing in oneself. One young pastor adamantly asserted, "The resurrection is the greatest miracle of all. How can you say that belief in yourself is the greatest miracle?" Simply put, the resurrection occurred for the sake of the person, not the person for the sake of the resurrection. Jesus had no intention of showing off His resurrection power for its own sake; instead, He rose from the dead so that all men and women might rise from the tomb of their own darkness and unconsciousness and into new life — a life filled with consciousness, faith, and belief in the self.

Since Jesus dwells within one's innermost self, personal confidence is, in actuality, faith in the overflowing providence of Jesus who realizes the importance of believing in oneself. To see with this much clarity is to move from blindness to sight. And then we, as the man born blind described in John's gospel, can proclaim, "All I know is that once I was blind but now I can see."

Healing for the People-Pleaser

A people-pleaser has no vision for his or her own life. Their own sense of self has been greatly damaged and in no way are they able to see their way clearly in life. Frequently, such people complain that they never have time for themselves. Indeed, they do not. They are possessed by the need to please others and are constantly working for approval and recognition.

One morning, right before waking, I had a most terrifying nightmare. The face of the Medusa presented herself before me. This feminine face with a multitude of snakes arising out of her head terrified me. I awoke with a start.

The next hour, during my morning prayer, I understood the meaning of this powerful image. The Medusa symbolized the entanglements, the unhealthy ties with people and pleasing people that had accumulated in my life. The multitude of snakes represented the many unhealthy ties that thwarted my own growth and development. Personally, I had already sensed this as a feeling of being held back, tied down, and oppressed by some unconscious force. Now, I knew that the Medusa had taken hold of me.

Two years of intense inner work was required to bring integration and healing to me. Unbeknownst to myself, these unhealthy ties and desires to please people had infected family relationships, ministry within the church, and my professional life as well. The desire to please others, even to the point of sacrificing my personal well-being, ran rampant within me. Indeed, it possessed me. It left me blind and unable to see my way clearly in life. Such a sickness of soul must be healed before one can fully live the life that God has created him or her to live.

To live one's own life requires inner strengthening and freedom from external entanglements. Accordingly, St. Paul prays:

> In the abundance of His glory, may He, through His spirit, enable you to grow firm in power with regard to your inner self, so that Christ may live in your hearts through faith, and then, planted in love and built on love, with all God's holy people, you will have the strength to grasp the breadth and the length, the height and the depth; so that, knowing the love of Christ, which is beyond knowledge, you may be filled with the utter fullness of God. (Eph 3:16–19)

Inner strengthening means developing a growing sense of interior firmness as one grows into greater communion with God.

Christ lives in the heart. As the heart is strengthened and made well, so self-confidence increases. A faith-filled life becomes the mainstay of one's existence. Love, real love — without gnarled ties and enmeshments — becomes possible. The soul is rooted in Christ and only in Christ. No one possesses such a person and he or she does not desire to possess anyone else. Christ is the Center of his or her life.

Many months after having initially encountered the symbol of the Medusa, I was required to address a large church gathering composed of a number of individuals who had openly expressed hostility toward some of my work and teaching. In the past, I had been tempted and had succumbed to the temptation to dilute my message on the inner life. At that point in my life, the Medusa had possessed me. Now, with greater consciousness, I felt I had another chance to be forthright and uncompromising with regard to who I was and what I was about.

As I entered the front of the auditorium, I noticed a display case featuring posters of upcoming civic events. At the center of the case, looming large at me, was the dated poster for a recently-held exhibit on ancient Carthage. Someone had forgotten to remove this month-old print. The picture, bold as could be, was that of the Medusa. Synchronistically, God's grace came to me as a reminder to stand fast in my freedom.

Toxic people-pleasing had crippled my life in so many ways. In the church, I felt compelled to say what others wanted to hear. The collective pressures of the group would inevitably seduce me. I strayed from Christ-centeredness and became addicted to pleasing the people of the church. This occurred gradually and over a period of many years. So subtle and devious was this tyranny, that I soon found myself depleted and quite unfulfilled spiritually. Only with the conscious awareness of the Medusa — the unhealthy ties to groups of various sorts — did I experience freedom and greater personal integration.

That evening after finishing my delivery, at least a dozen individuals walked up to me and thanked me for being so direct. Needless to say, I too felt grateful. I knew, and continue to know, the critical importance of being healed of people-pleasing, a form of the messiah/martyr complex. It is good when others can relate to me and I can relate to them; however, I no longer feel the compulsion to please all of the people all of the time. All that is necessary is to grow firm in grace in your innermost self so that Christ might live in your heart through faith.

The "Don't Talk" Curse

Following on the heels of the "don't feel" curse and the "don't trust" curse is the "don't talk" curse. A family inculcates its members with the belief that talking about troublesome feelings is unacceptable and will not be tolerated. Thus, family members exchange only superficial ideas and notions with each other. Depth of communication is avoided at all costs.

Such a family creates rage-aholics. People who cannot talk become rage-ridden people. The human being needs to express deeply-held thoughts and feelings. Without being able to do so, emotional toxicity runs rampant in the soul. Rage results when talking is suppressed.

The unity of the family, whether the church family or the nuclear family, is devastated when talking is prohibited. No real person-to-person understanding ever takes place. People only help to maintain the status quo and diligently avoid rocking the boat. By talking about honest concerns, the equilibrium, the status quo would be upset. Rather than risk this, no one talks and no one is permitted to talk.

If a family member ventures forth and expresses his or her beliefs or deeply held feelings, he or she is quickly shunned. This often takes the form of quickly looking the other way or completely disregarding the stated verbal message. They may be snubbed by other family members. Others might walk away from them. In some cases, they are treated as oddities, eccentrics, or perhaps even considered to be crazy.

The truthful person then has a decision to make. Either they leave their family, religious community, or other group that is fostering the "don't talk" curse, or they deny their feelings and give in to the pressure not to communicate. In so doing, they will gradually become, more and more, rage-aholics. They will notice themselves meeting frustrating events that inevitably occur in everyone's life, with rage. Outbursts of temper and even uncontrollable fits, could potentially plague their day-to-day life. In a manner of speaking, craziness will set in. To not talk means to violate nature and, when nature is violated, payment is demanded. A crime has been committed. This crime is a crime against the soul. The penalty is a lack of emotional and spiritual vitality — sickness of soul cripples such a one.

Face It

The first step the rage-aholic needs to take in dealing with this form of spiritual possession, is to face it. As an alcoholic admits his alcoholism, so a rage-aholic must face the fact that rage has become overpowering. Anger can no longer be dealt with in a normal and healthy manner. It builds and builds until it explodes. Such an admission by a rage-aholic is the first step towards recovery.

Without such an admission, the rage-aholic may attempt to force-fully control his or her expressions of anger. This only contributes to internal disintegration. They then become angrier and angrier with themselves. Interior unity and equanimity is thus further destroyed as the rage-aholic attempts to overpower this awesome compulsion.

Inner unity can be promoted only as one surrenders to Jesus and faces the fact that rage has become master of the house. "Take every effort to preserve the unity of the Spirit by the peace that binds you together" (Eph 4:3). Yielding to the inner experience of Jesus settles one into a more tranquil state of receptivity. Grace then operates where willpower alone would never suffice. Surrendering to God, together with prayerful self-realization and spiritual direction or psychotherapy, assist the sufferer to face long-held feelings of rage. Only in this is peace to be found.

A saint of old expounds on breaking ties with all that encumbers and tyrannizes the soul:

Oh my God, whatever is nearer to me than Thou, things of this
earth, and things more naturally pleasing to me...keep Thou my
eyes, my ears, my heart, from any such miserable tyranny. Break
my bonds — raise my heart. Keep my whole being fixed on Thee.
Let me never lose sight of Thee; and, while I gaze on Thee, let my
love of Thee grow more and more every day.

A rage-aholic confided:

In my childhood, I was constantly reprimanded with, 'Children are
to be seen and not heard.' I learned never to talk, especially about
anything that troubled me or angered me. During my teenage
years, I was known to have a temper. Others were shocked. I
seemed to be meek and mild and yet, out of the blue and when least
expected, I would explode.

After many months of marital counseling, we witnessed a gradual
settling of soul come over him. By facing his rage, he came to understand his anger. Forced by the possible dissolution of his marriage, he
came to terms with the demon of rage. He learned to face and to feel his
anger appropriately. In turn, he experienced greater interior peace and
marital harmony. He concluded a particular psychotherapy session by
saying, "I don't explode now because I am able to be angry when I need
to be."

For the rage-aholic, the facing of anger and the feeling of anger are
all important. An intellectual understanding and admission of one's
angry feelings is not sufficient. One must be willing to fully feel the
depth and intensity of angry feelings. This is not to say that one gives
way to outbursts of temper and tirades of rage; this is the behavior of a
rage-aholic. Rather, anger, faced and felt, is actually a very reflective
undertaking.

With depth of anger, an individual requires time in order to arrive
at an understanding of underlying motives and causes. It takes time
to understand one's anger. It can be expressed verbally if done in a
respectful and forthright manner. However, the key element is to grow in
self-understanding as the result of facing and feeling anger.

St. Paul exhorts, "Even if you are angry, do not sin; never let the
sun set on your anger or else you will give the devil a foothold" (Eph
4:26). The Greek mind always considered three different types of anger:
quick temper, bitterness, and righteous indignation. A quick temper is
sinful in that it is egocentric and motivated by a desire to maintain one's

defensive style of living that can be quite hurtful to self and others. Bitterness is sinful in that one dwells on past hurts to the point of cultivating feelings of self-pity and even retribution. Righteous indignation is a form of anger that St. Paul does not consider sinful in that it is an aggressive assertion that maintains the integrity of the self.

Jesus angrily threw the money changers out of the temple asserting, "My house shall be called a house of prayer." St. Paul angrily parted ways with Barnabas when he felt that some of his fundamental values had been violated. I remember angrily confronting the parents of one of my teenage patients: "If you do not help her to get the therapy that she needs, and stop discouraging her, you may feel miserable for quite a long time, especially if she attempts suicide." Shocked, confronted with the seriousness of their daughter's pain, they began driving her to therapy rather than making her walk two miles, and encouraging her rather than criticizing the process of psychotherapy.

I remember that after this young girl and I worked together for two years, we both sensed a very deep satisfaction. She commented, "I was stunned when you became so angry with my parents. They never wanted to cross you again. It sure helped to get the point across. It helped to make me healthier. Now, when I feel angry, I talk about it. I don't yell and scream. I just talk like we are talking now. I feel good and I feel healthy."

To suppress talking delivers powerful insult to the psyche. In fact, it can potentially render it quite unhealthy. The ability to communicate one's deepest feelings is a *sine qua non* for the spiritual life. With it, growth gradually and surely takes place; without it, one's interior life turns stale, stagnant, and out of sorts.

This is not to decry the value and importance of silence. Appropriate silence nourishes the soul. However, silence used as a means of escaping from feelings and people disintegrates true spirituality. The meaningfulness of silence emerges from the way in which it enriches one's capacity for feeling and thus for knowing God.

In this sense, not only is silence holy but conversation becomes holy when it is a rendering of heartfelt emotion. It is a way of experiencing God. When two individuals talk together, each listening to the other, each expressing his or her own self, God is with them. When two or three gather in His name, He is present. To be together in His name calls for intimacy and honest exchange between individuals — Jesus is as alive in such a moment as He was when He walked the streets of Nazareth.

As one begins the process of breaking away from the family curse of not talking, equanimity of souls settles in. In the place of rage, outbursts of temper and general disquietude, a greater union with one's own soul becomes evident. The person feels at peace with himself or herself. Throughout the course of one's life, as the years pass, one is more and more able to confide intimacies with those who truly understand, with those who themselves have cut the ties of their own family curse. In these relationships anger, rather than being a curse, unfolds as a blessing that helps to maintain the integrity of caring relationships and the individuality of the soul.

Moaners And Groaners

For every rage-aholic, there is an accompanying messiah/martyr complex that we will refer to as the moaning and groaning way. Those possessed by moaning and groaning believe they must suffer at the hands of the rage-aholic. Indeed, they often view it as their plight in life to "save" tormented and enraged souls. They frequently enter into marriage with the idea of changing their spouse. Quite often, Christians go so far as to consider this to be God's will for their life.

The rage-aholic does not talk about his or her anger; rather, rage is vomited up, released, and relief is sought. The moaner and groaner is the one person in the rage-aholic's life that permits himself or herself to be dumped on and used. Without such a person, the rage-aholic would have to confront the horror of personal pain. Therefore, the moaner and groaner, in a non-redemptive manner, suffers the misery of the rage-aholic so as to provide a modicum of relief for the rage-aholic and therein continual misery for himself or herself. Such a messiah is quite a forlorn person.

Without much happiness in life, a messiah seems to constantly exude a quality of moaning and groaning in the midst of life's circumstances. This is understandable since they are not carrying their own cross, but choose instead to be the brunt of the rage-aholic's torment. They moan and groan under such a weighty and preposterous burden. Who wouldn't groan with malaise when carrying the weight of the world, the rage of the world, on one's shoulders?

Frequently, a martyr is greatly esteemed in the church. He or she may even be referred to as a long-suffering saint. What is missed here is the egocentricity of their position. Not only does the martyr complex shield the rage-aholic from facing inner pain, it also keeps the moaner and groaner so preoccupied by the rage-aholic that personal neurosis is never addressed. Defensiveness and egocentricity characterize the way of the moaners and groaners. They are so taken up by others that they never find their own personal way. It can be seen, therefore, that the way of the moaner and groaner is undeniably egocentric and definitely not Christlike.

In order to emerge from this abhorrent and awful toxicity, the moaner and groaner must leave behind the expectations of others to put up with rage. Together with this, it is necessary to face and work through personal guilt with regard to allowing the rage-aholic to now deal with his or her own life. In other words, the martyr must be willing to forego egocentricity in favor of truly following Jesus. Such a decision begins the process of detaching one's self from the rage-aholic and facing the dark side of one's own nature. Healing grace is then free to flow and liberate one from the clutches of this messiah/martyr complex.

An essential hallmark of a happy and functional family is seen in the ability not only to communicate forthrightly, but also to refrain from exploiting weaknesses in other members. In other words, unhappy families composed of, perhaps, many moaners and groaners, exploit each other's weaknesses. In some instances, a person may be both a rage-aholic and a martyr, sometimes looking for others who will permit the dumping of their rage and, at other times, permitting themselves to be dumped upon.

At the Syracuse University College for Human Development, Alice Honig, Ph.D., notes that family members either tear each other down or build each other up. Family life then proceeds in either a "vicious cycle" (tearing down) or in a "virtuous cycle" (building up). She explains, "In unhappy families, everyone provides constant alarms to make each other tense and upset and distressed. Each child and each adult knows the other's weak spots and they know how to shame and embarrass each other."

Dr. Honig continues, "In happy families, the same principle works in reverse. Whether it's remembering to write an anniversary card or striving for good marks in school, each person can figure out what they can do to make the others pleased and happy. They learn to accommodate each other and to make each other comfortable."

The difference between unhappiness and happiness in the family, therefore, can be seen in whether members choose to understand and encourage each other or opt to exploit and belittle one another. The rage-aholic and the martyr find different outlets for their egocentricities in the unhappy family. Both are nestled comfortably away from their own pain and thereby inflict it on others. Ironically enough, this precipitates intense personal misery for both the rage-aholic and the martyr rather than bearing any sort of lasting potential for relief. Real healing issues forth from facing, not inflicting, pain.

Be Healed; Be Whole; Be Well

> Do not grieve the Holy Spirit of God who has marked you with His seal, ready for the day when we shall be set free. Any bitterness or bad temper or anger or shouting or abuse must be far removed from you — as must every kind of malice. Be generous to one another, sympathetic, forgiving each other as readily as God forgave you in Christ. (Eph 4:30–32)

St. Paul moves the reader toward healing by creating a sensitivity toward grieving the Holy Spirit of God and creating an alertness toward a potential for authentic God-inspired forgiveness.

Inevitably, the suffering martyr experiences great internal malice. In this, the Holy Spirit dwelling within the soul is, so to speak, deeply offended. That is to say, malice shatters unity with the soul and God. It consumes one's energy and intentions, moving the heart away from Jesus-centered living. Malicious ways of injuring the rage-aholic are dwelt upon. Such thoughts consume the martyr, even though they are rarely acted out, at least in an active manner.

The one afflicted by a martyr complex may passively hurt the rage-aholic. Through seemingly innocuous yet maiming statements, through forgetfulness, slips of the tongue, and a variety of other nonchalant insults, the rage of the martyr leaks out. All to no avail, this incessant stream of passive rage cripples the spiritual life and, at least temporarily, blocks growth.

God-inspired forgiveness comes from the martyr realizing that unhealthy passivity, stemming from low self-esteem, has carved out their horrible niche in life. The rage-aholic is not to blame for the suffering of the martyr. This moaner and groaner need only take up the cross, face his or her own unresolved rage, in order to know firsthand God's forgiving and healing touch.

Once this is done, the moaner and groaner gradually senses a divinely inspired forgiveness toward the rage-aholic. This forgiveness ushers them away from the role of suffering martyr and helps them to maintain an appropriate distance from rage-aholics. True, the former martyr forgives the rage-aholic, but at the same time the recovering moaner and groaner no longer subjects himself or herself to the rage-aholic's outbursts. Love and forgiveness are real and are felt — from a distance.

One woman candidly reflected:

> I finally told my husband one day, "I don't want to hear about it." For too long I had been putting up with his ranting and raving. Through psychotherapy and my personal spiritual devotions, I gained strength to put an end to the matter. I literally pointed my finger at him whenever he would start his temper tantrums, and would say, "I don't want to hear about it." It left him stunned and shocked.
>
> I'm sure this is not a formula for everyone, but it has worked for me. It only took a dozen times or so before he realized that I was not going to budge. In fact, I had already made up my mind to leave him if he did not respond. I felt with certainty that God did not intend me to be abused emotionally. It has now been three years since my husband's last outburst of temper. He knew that I would not put up with it any longer.
>
> I didn't count on this, but he himself decided to enter psychotherapy. Once I was no longer the dumping ground for his rage, he was left with no other alternative but to deal with it himself. I guess he could have opted to handle it in some negative manner such as through alcoholism or adultery but, through the grace of God, he chose psychotherapy. I'm not sure what is going on for him during his therapy since it's between him and his psychotherapist, but I do know that he seems more settled. By withdrawing from being a martyr, I actually ended up helping him. This was not my intent, but it sure turned out to be a nice by-product of my resolve. As far as his bad temper was concerned, he couldn't take it out on me any longer, so he chose to work it out.

Of fundamental importance for the martyr is the wholehearted decision to be healed, to be whole, to be well. Without the yielding of egocentricities such as self-pity and the sympathy gained from others, no healing can take place. Forsaking the rewards associated with being a martyr means to embrace potential for life.

Jesus, at the pool called Bethesda, asked the paralytic, "Do you want to be well again?" Interestingly, the man did not answer affirmatively; he complained that he had no one to put him into the pool, he groaned that others got into the water before him. Jesus completely bypassed his martyr complex and said, "Get up, pick up your sleeping mat and walk around." The man was instantly healed. Instead of being grateful, this man grumbled against Jesus to the Jews, an act that helped to incite the Jewish leaders to harass and eventually kill Jesus.

Jesus, the Center of your being, beckons you to leave behind your illness, your comfortable mat of moaning and groaning. In its place, He promises healing, wellness, wholeness. To leave behind the past is difficult, for it requires separating from what has grown to be quite comfortable. Some, as the paralytic mentioned in the scriptures, would even prefer ill health to living a responsible and authentic life. The choice is not easy. Jesus heals the family curse. Jesus is a healing Jesus for moaners and groaners. Jesus calls to you: "Be healed, be whole, be well."

The "Don't Grow" Curse

As with the other curses, the "don't grow" curse aims at thwarting human maturation and development. More specifically, however, the "don't grow" curse aims at killing the individual's desire for unique expression and creativity. The family invests time, energy, and effort at crippling any member who wants to grow past what are considered to be accepted family values and norms. Herein, the way the family operates is the way the individual should operate and, if not, the family will attempt to maim the one seeking growth.

In such cases, the particular family member feels weighted down and unable to see "the forest for the trees." Actually, the mob of the family has superceded the aspirations of the individual in favor of group control and domination. The individual psychologically bound and imprisoned cannot see his or her way clear. Unless he or she is freed, such a thwarted individual remains forever emotionally immature and dwarfed.

If growth is attempted, it is met with explicit or implicit messages such as, "You think you're too good for us." "What's happened to you?" "Don't you like us anymore?" "You used to be just one of the gang, now you're too uppity for us." "Love begins at home and you sure aren't treating us very well."

All of these messages convey a curse that asserts, "We're miserable and we want you to remain with us so that we can all be miserable together." Undeniably, the force of the family curse is strong; indeed, at times, overwhelming. An individual can literally lose his or her soul to the family. The kingdom of heaven calls for continued growth, not stagnation. I have often said that the spiritual life is like an airplane flying through the sky: "If you stop, you drop." The meaning of this is that spirituality beckons the believer to constantly die to egocentricities and live to Christ. Without this ever on-going process, the soul dries up and decays.

In other words, there is no such thing as spiritual stagnation. One either grows or dies. Growth necessitates inner confrontation with one's dark side. This may separate one from others who wish to remain unconscious. Through all generations, Christ's message remains clear: "Wake up, O Sleeper, rise from the dead and Christ will shine on you" (Eph 5:14).

Don't Give Up

Thwarted growth can cause feelings of despair and gloom to quickly paralyze the soul. Since she was made for growth, the soul always reacts adversely to stifling attitudes and entanglements. An individual may sense himself or herself being "out of sorts," no longer in touch with soul. This is, indeed, a very precarious and dangerous situation for the consequences can be quite painful.

Disorders of soul may be symbolized physically. That is to say, a hurting soul may be reflected in a hurting body. Since the body and soul were meant to work together, the well-being or unrest of one affects the other. An ill soul can create a diseased body.

A recent medical publication estimated that ninety percent of all physical disorders were rooted in the psyche. Despite the fact that this percentage may seem a bit exaggerated, it is regarded as a conservative estimate. The following physical ills were listed as being significantly affected and perhaps even caused by psychological issues: accident proneness, allergies and asthma, angina, arthritis, back pain, cancer, child health problems, cold and canker sores, dental cavities, epilepsy, gum disease, hair and scalp problems, headaches, heart disease, hemophilia, high blood pressure, insomnia, impotence and sexual dysfunction, irritable bowel syndrome, pelvic pain, pregnancy problems, skin problems, and ulcers.

Of course definite physical contributors can quite often be found for each of these diseases. However, with thorough investigation, it seems as though emotional factors also play a significant role. Unresolved feelings that impinge on human growth may generate such internal tension that the body breaks down. One person may find himself or herself to be genetically susceptible to heart disease, another disposed by family history to cancer, and someone else might develop arthritis given the right psychological climate. Always, physical medicine and psychotherapy must work together to effect relief and, hopefully, a cure.

When a person suffers from toxic curses, family entanglements, and suppressed emotions, he or she may find release through physical illness. Nothing is resolved, but the message is clear that he or she has lost touch with the soul. Only by delving deeply within, facing one's dark side, and disentangling from the "don't grow" curse will the potential for physical health be maximized.

A psychotherapeutic relationship, or intensive spiritual direction, can provide hope for the afflicted and despairing soul that has known the ravages of physical disease. Such inertia and lethargy plague the victim of the "don't grow" curse so that he or she desperately needs a hope-filled relationship. Working together with one who has traveled the inner way brings healing to soul and body. Through the labyrinth of interior darkness and light, the sufferer must proceed in order to find true freedom from the curse and the everlasting hope fulfilled in time and space of Christ bestowing blessing: "...and Christ will shine on you."

Healing for the Sick-aholic

People who have been thwarted in their spiritual and psychological growth may, as we have previously noted, become physically ill. In some cases, they become messiah/martyr "sick-aholics." Often, quite unconsciously, sickness enables the individual psychically to carry the suffering of the family. In so doing, it is wrongly believed that all will be made well in the family or community.

A very dramatic example of this occurred during my residency program. When consulting for an oncology unit in the medical complex, I happened to visit a seven-year-old boy dying of cancer. I asked him how he was doing and quite surprisingly he answered, "I know I'm going to die, but that's alright. Ever since I've been sick, Mom and Dad don't fight anymore. They never fight when I'm sick. So, I guess it's alright if I die. That means that they'll never fight again."

Needless to say, I left his hospital room in shock. In his mind, he had sacrificed his life for the well-being of his parents' marriage. Quite innocently, he felt that if sickness brought a temporary end to their fighting, then death would stop their fighting forever. Unconsciously, sickness served the function of creating suffering for one so that the many, ostensibly, would be well. Of course, this is never a true solution since one person cannot work out another's problems.

This seven-year-old boy symbolically incorporated the conflict between his parents. As his parents tore into each other, so the cancer devoured him. In point of fact, the boy himself was being eaten alive by the rage between his parents. Parents must pay heed to chronic sickness in their children for it may be indicative of unresolved marital discord. As parents realize the power of a child's psyche to symbolically portray their marital relationship, greater depths of understanding, parent to parent and parent to child, can be achieved.

Let Go of a Curse — Take Hold of a Blessing

Curses inevitably lead to blessings as one understands their symbolic meaning. To let go of a curse necessitates relinquishing unhealthy attachments to the person who has forwarded the curse. This may implicate parents, long-held relationships with seeming friends, or relationships of other sorts. All need to be counted as relinquished if one truly desires to be touched by the Healer.

A young Catholic nun told me of her agony in dealing with her parents.

> I decided to go home and pay them a visit during the holidays. I always told myself that I looked forward to our time spent together. Once I began psychotherapy, however, I soon understood that many dark feelings toward my parents lurked within me. I was conflicted about whether to see my parents for what they truly were.
>
> Once I arrived at their home, my eyes began bothering me. The condition became so severe that an ophthalmologist bandaged them for almost the entire duration of my stay. In order to avoid exacerbating this eye disease, he placed patches over both eyes. My parents literally had to lead me around as long as I remained with them.
>
> Fortunately, I recovered from this disease and realized its symbolic meaning. My parents had never been warm or respectful as I would have liked them to be. In fact, they are rather cold and dominating. I did not want to see the truth. I always felt that seeing my parents as perfect enabled me to honor them and so treat them in a Christian manner. Now, I believe honoring my parents comes naturally when I see them for what they are. I am aware of their strengths and limitations and so, I adjust my relating to them accordingly. I no longer expect more of them than they can reasonably give. And, at the same time, I do not expect myself to give more than I can reasonably give to them.

I fought against seeing my parents clearly. My eye disease perfectly symbolized this. In refusing to see them clearly, I inadvertently allowed them to run my life. I then would become like a little girl being led around by her parents. I am no longer a little girl. I am a grown woman and I honor my parents by seeing them clearly.

The scriptural injunction to honor your father and mother so that you may have long life and prosper in the land has been greatly misinterpreted. Parents use this text in an egocentric fashion to support their own manipulation and control over their children. When Christian parents want their adult children to behave in a certain manner, or maintain a particular attitude, they may quote this text feeling that it gives them biblical support for unquestioned authority. I know of innumerable instances where Christian adults have been beaten into submission with this text by their supposedly Christian parents.

To honor father and mother, in actuality, enjoins the adult to correctly understand his or her parents. In modern jargon, this translates as "to understand where they're coming from." This enables the adult to relate with appropriate kindness, courtesy, and integrity toward parents. It involves mutual respect and encouragement toward individual growth and independence. Honoring another person excludes all forms of blind submission, tyranny, and manipulation. Health of mind, body, and soul abound as parents respect children and children respect parents.

As a curse gives way to blessing, integration and independence develop. This may translate into greater physical health. The toxic enmeshment of the "don't grow" curse bottles up unhealthy emotions and creates such an extraordinary psychological pressure that physical ailments may result. The abatement of this tension, through working out the curse, fortifies the individual with strength in the place of debilitation. Health, rather than sickness, accompanies, more and more, the one who discovers deliverance from family curses.

After a bible study, a middle-aged woman hesitantly told me her story. Briefly, taking no more than five minutes, she encapsulated her torment and recovery. For so many years, she suffered intense stomach pains and indigestion whenever she spoke with her mother. Whether visiting her home or talking on the phone, an encounter with her mother left her uptight, nauseated, and pained.

She related:

> I am now a fifty-three-year-old woman and still my mother tells me what to do and how to do it. Without a thought, she criticizes my dress, my eating habits and even my speech. She demands first place in my life regardless of my obligations to my own children. In her eyes, I have been and will always be her little girl.
>
> I am not sure how I came to it, but one morning, I decided that enough was enough. I felt so angry with her that I couldn't take it anymore. When she called me that morning, I immediately placed my hand over my belly button and mentally told myself I am my own woman and a separate person from my mother. After doing this a number of times, I felt marvelously disconnected from her. I have grown to speak forthrightly and directly to her. At first, she was very offended, so I kept my distance from her for a while so that she could get used to the new me. Gradually she became more respectful and less intrusive. Now I see her less frequently than I used to, but when I do see her, we are respectful and courteous with one another. By the way, I can't remember the last time I felt stomach troubles of any sort. When I let go of my mother, I let go of my stomach pains.

Healing the family curse demands that the individual be willing to wholeheartedly pursue interior growth. To find release from negative ways of living, one must often be willing to release negative people. Continuing through life with harmful relationships only serves to nurture an already operative curse. Unhealthy people generate unhealthy relationships. Letting go of unhealthy people and relationships is a requisite for the healing of the family curse.

Such a road is not an easy one to travel. We all grow complacent and comfortable in the status quo. It is not without reason that Jesus stated that believers must forsake all and follow Him. The inner way to follow Jesus wholeheartedly is a task that calls forth great courage and perseverance. Without such a radical commitment, one may superficially state that he or she desires healing but in fact departs from the inner way once pain surfaces. Many are called but few respond.

The few who shoulder the cross of daily life in such a way that inner transformation takes place will enter into a more and more profound and loving relationship with the Risen Christ. Together with this, healthy relationships will gradually be reestablished. The process is a gradual one, and at times causes the individual to feel quite alone. But in and through reliance on Him, the soul learns the inner way — a way of deliverance from the family curse. To sacrifice all, to follow the interior way of healing, means to follow the way of the few and hear His interior promptings, to live His interior inspirations, to let go of the curse and take hold of a blessing.

Six

The Jesus Cure

In the last analysis, the cure for religious neurosis involves encountering the reality of the Risen Jesus. Done not only once, through a life-changing spiritual experience, but lived daily through continual self-reflection and yielding to the Holy Spirit, authentic spiritual experience leads one into real life. The Jesus cure, then, refers to knowing the reality of Jesus firsthand in all dimensions of life. Such an awakening constitutes a spiritual conversion of the deepest kind in which God is perceived to be all and in all.

Life becomes unitary as opposed to segmented. Rather than perceiving harsh lines dividing the sacred and the secular, the Holy Spirit's presence pervades all things. One may opt to use certain situations in an egocentric manner, but still the potential in that situation is one of latent goodness and wholeness that can contribute to the well-being of humankind. Having been touched by Jesus, the soul now yearns to engage in life fully, both for the benefit of oneself and others. Life is approached from the perspective of optimism rather than pessimism, knowing that in one way or another God is always at work.

The Jesus cure translates into the deepest possible cure for the ailing human condition. It affects one on the physical, emotional, and spiritual planes. Living in tune and in harmony with Him settles one into a new lifestyle. All that creates toxic disharmony and chaos is forsaken. That which nurtures inner harmony with Him and thus betters one's creative capabilities in life is sought out and adhered to. In positively affecting and healing all areas of life by first healing the soul, the Jesus cure leaves one widely awake to the fullness and freshness of life.

I am convinced that many individuals have experienced the Jesus cure without ever making a formal and evangelical proclamation of faith. For one reason or another, people can be repulsed by institutionalized religion and what they consider to be contrived means of religious observance and faith. Nonetheless, I have found that often those of sincere heart who honestly seek truth encounter the reality of Jesus. They adamantly refuse to identify with denominational stances or dogmatic positions. However, it is uncontested, in my opinion, that their spiritual experience of healing and transformation is an undeniable encounter with the Risen Jesus as evidenced by their markedly transformed attitudes, relationships, and life in general.

God is so big that His touch upon the human soul is not confined to the preconceptions of human beings. He may work within denominational structures or may choose, for whatever reason, to intervene in a human life without the agency of an institution or specified manner of approaching Him. God's only desire is to love and heal the human heart. As institutions and denominations facilitate this purpose, then God will work through them; otherwise, He will work in many and diverse ways to bring the hurting soul to Himself and minister tenderly and lovingly through His healing grace.

The Blind Spot — The Cure

The healing of souls depends weightedly on one central factor: the ability to see one's blind spot. In reality, there are many such blind spots. These consist of facets of one's personality that are unconscious, not within one's awareness. Others close to you may be quite clear with regard to your faults and hidden potentials. But to you they remain concealed: these are your blind spots.

These blind spots are not of a solely negative nature. Virtues as well as vices may be hidden from one's conscious awareness. Such unconsciousness fosters difficulties of one sort or another. At the very least, unconsciousness hampers personal growth and development. All too often, it arouses problems and discord aplenty.

As blind spots are faced and dealt with, fullness of life ensues. Jesus proclaimed, "The thief comes only to steal and kill and destroy. I have come so that they may have life and have it to the full" (Jn 10:10). Unconsciousness steals and destroys life. Consciousness, the light of Christ shining in the deepest recesses of the soul, imbues the soul with fullness of life manifesting itself in a healthy and creative existence.

Whenever darkness, dryness, tiredness, and hopelessness beset the soul, it can be almost definitely surmised that one is caught in the grip of an unconscious inner force. This hidden away attitude or feeling drains away vitality and zest. Only through prayerful self-reflection will this underlying darkness be exposed. It often contains the seeds of new growth and blessing. Creative possibilities open up as the once oppressive inner darkness is forthrightly faced and understood.

One evening, just prior to arriving home after a full day's work, I noticed myself feeling somewhat grouchy and irritable. I realized that to leave this mood unattended could prove hazardous for the evening, as any of us are likely to take out our moodiness on those that we love. Rather than doing this, I chose to quiet myself and reflect on the day's proceedings, to see what might be unconsciously distressing me.

After finishing my regular jog and sitting quietly, alone, on my front steps, a thought came to mind. Earlier that day I had been informed that the mother general of a very large religious order had referred to me as a "pompous ass." Upon hearing this, I quickly dismissed what I considered to be a bigoted and baseless opinion. However, secretly it distressed me.

That evening, after dinner, I confided to my wife, Kathy, my concern. A number of months prior, this mother general had contacted me with regard to the psychotherapeutic treatment of some of her sisters. At first, she lent her encouragement and support. Later, she practically demanded details with regard to the nuns I was seeing. I adamantly refused her request and firmly stated that I regarded the consultation of psychotherapy to be as sacred as the confessional. I would not betray the confidence of the individuals I was seeing. She curtly asked if I was telling her that the details of psychotherapy were none of her business. I resounded heartily in the affirmative that the details of psychotherapy were in fact none of her business. Her business was to provide support and encouragement for the sisters while they were undergoing psychotherapy. Without a further word, she ended our conversation by hanging up the telephone. Later, I found out that she had held this refusal against me and cast disparaging remarks my way.

Once I opened up to my wife and I vulnerably saw my blind spot, the former irritability subsided. I realized that I felt unappreciated and misunderstood. Many times before I had assisted this mother general and gone out of my way for her. She was, in fact, taking my services and consultation with her for granted. To admit that I felt slighted, used, and hurt helped to set me free. Without "seeing," I would have continued to carry this irritability on into the evening, making for an uncomfortable situation for both me and my family. Instead, the light of understanding was able to shine on personal discontent and bring with it the fruit of deepened understanding and sensitivity between my wife, my family, and myself.

I remember when Tom, a hunched-over, distraught-looking middle-aged man, arrived at my office for his first consultation. He complained of severe misery and depression. When I asked him the reason for his woes, he immediately retorted, "It's all my wife's fault. She just doesn't love me in the way that I need to be loved. If she was a better wife, I wouldn't feel this way."

Common to all who are ignorant of their blind spots is blame. If only some situation or person would be different, then all would be well, says the blamer. Self-reflection and prayerful introspection are foreign to such a one, since outer answers for inner problems are forever sought.

After many months of working together, Tom finally admitted:

> I am seeing more and more that the fact of my father's death when I was only five years old, together with my mother's alcoholism throughout my teenage years, definitely wounded me. I was left feeling that no one really loved me or ever would love me. I think I have really been depressed ever since I was a child. It's not my wife's fault that I feel this way. It's time that I took responsibility for my own misery and depression. I have to deal with my own feelings, because no one else is going to do it for me.

After approximately eighteen months of working together, Tom was given a job transfer to a neighboring state. Since his course of psychotherapy had not been completed, I encouraged him to follow through with treatment with another Christian psychologist in his city. At the end of our last session together, Tom commented:

> I know that I have more work to do but one thing is for sure: I can't blame anyone for my predicament. Psychotherapy is helping me to learn how to love and be loved. Now, whenever I start feeling the old sense of depression, I realize that I am somehow cutting myself off from love. Depression is a signal for me that I need love. No one is to blame. It's just something that I have to realize and work with. I am going to make it.

Tom's clear-minded attitude toward his toxic depression came only after many months of painstaking truth-facing. The Jesus cure always necessitates facing one's unconscious attitudes and feelings — one's blind spots. In the healing light of Christ, such inner discoveries liberate the soul from the tyranny of unconsciousness. God is a god of light, of consciousness, and all who follow Him must follow Him in the light.

How to Lighten Your Load

To be intimately acquainted with the fullness of life offers one the opportunity to carry a lighter load. Often, however, life's labors are such that a heavy heart can easily weigh one down. Without thinking, individuals yield to negative and toxic attitudes that oppress the spirit. Letting go of such negative and destructive elements, all attitudes that run counter to interior wholeness and freedom, liberates the soul into fullness of life.

The Gospel of John states, "In Him was life, life that was the light of men; and light shines in darkness, and darkness could not overpower it" (Jn 1:3–5). Life offers light. Light exposes all that threatens to over-power the soul with darkness and death. Such exposure brings healing and health.

The Jesus cure calls us into light. Living one's life in the light releases untold potentialities and graces. Jesus heals every wound and lifts every burden as light, His light, permeates one's innermost being.

To live in the light means acquiring new realizations and understand-ings with regard to oneself, to others, and to the situation at hand. To always see things in the same old way digs us into a rut. We then become comfortable in the old way of seeing things and doing things. This blocks the flow of God's grace. God desires to pour forth an ever fresh and ever new grace into life. The Jesus cure creates fresh grace for new problems.

Life's unexpected difficulties usually cannot be solved by maintain-ing worn-out and rigid attitudes. For a person to steadfastly keep used up and tired out approaches that may have worked in the past but are no longer viable betrays great insecurity. Only by a genuine willingness to yield to the new, to God-in-the-now, does Jesus and the fullness of His power and light freely act.

The inner power of Jesus propels the soul out of ruts. It literally takes a shaking up, often in the form of life crises, to shake loose destructive ideas and approaches. To propel us out of the ruts, God allows us to clearly see just what a jam we're in. We often feel that we can sink no lower. When all seems hopeless and our old attitudes are defunct, new grace can pour into the soul and into the predicament. New realizations and understandings, deeper insights, surface at this point. The light overcomes the darkness. Now out of the rut, the soul feels a lighter load, an uplifted heart, and a newness of life.

Lighten Your Load

The perception of carrying a heavy load, a feeling that life is too hard, indicates the presence of a toxic conflict. That is to say, very uncon-sciously, the individual harbors discordant thoughts and feelings, and they are wearing him or her out. Long held and unresolved conflict drains away energy and depresses emotions.

In order to resolve conflict, light must shine on unconscious sentiments. Once this happens, the soul feels freed from heavy heartedness. The Jesus cure, in and through the light of consciousness, lightens life's load.

On Tuesday of last week, I noticed myself feeling very tired and heavy hearted. I arrived home for my afternoon jog and continued to feel quite sluggish. I wondered if I needed more rest, if I had been working too hard, or if I might even be suffering from the flu. Suddenly, as I was lacing up my jogging shoes, the word "conflict" was written across my mind.

In a flash of understanding, I saw that I had been experiencing conflict over a particular family matter. The children recently expressed their desire to stay at home during the holidays and enjoy a quieter Christmas. Usually, we were caught up in visiting relative after relative during the holidays. This left us exasperated and even depleted during what should be a very restful and relaxing family season.

I knew that I too wanted to settle into Christmas with my own family. However, I felt the pull of the extended family to carry on with the way things had always been. The conflict over this matter was unconsciously eating at me. In a matter of ten seconds all of this became clear.

With this light, I felt a definite decisiveness to do what was best for my own family. This resolve left me free and full of energy. I enjoyed the rest of the day, on into the evening with my family. The light of Christ sets us free — conflict free.

Lift Up Your Heart

Sometimes we are down so low that we feel quite forsaken and despairing. At times like this, nothing short of a miraculous intervention, propelling us out of the rut can dislodge the stumbling block of meaningless toxic depression. Once we have had enough, we usually turn to God with all of our might, and then He lifts us up and out of the dark pit of hopelessness.

One evening my son Paul told the family about how the Seneca Indians claimed to raise the dead back to life. The Indians would gather together the bones of the deceased and place them in a circle. Then, they would erect a teepee over the bones. They would then take to felling a very large tree next to the teepee. Right before the tree crashed down on the teepee, all of the Indians would yell out, "Run for your life, or the tree will smash you." It is reputed that the bones would jump up, reconnect, and out would run the formerly deceased person — fully alive and just in the nick of time.

The mood of depression so deadens the soul that a near crisis may often be required to stir one out of such doldrums. A contemplative Benedictine monk confided:

> Dr. DeBlassie, I know you believe that God speaks to men and women through dreams. After many months of doubting my vocation to contemplation and prayer, God's light finally shone through for me. Many months before, I encountered horrible doubts with regard to the efficacy of my ministry of prayer. I wondered if I should be engaging in a more practical ministry with more visible effects in people's lives. I actually considered leaving the monastery in order to be involved in a more practical work. Before doing so, my spiritual director and I decided to pray intensely for three days about this matter.
>
> I was so moody and depressed that it was actually hard for me to pray during these three days. Normally I find prayer to be quite natural and easy. During these three days, I yielded my vocation to God. Whatever He wanted me to do, I was willing to do.
>
> At the end of the three days, a dream came to me. I was standing right in the middle of St. Peter's Basilica in Rome. On the main altar I stood. The Holy Father approached me, looking radiant, filled with light. He embraced me and whispered, "Your prayer is the heart of the church." I awoke. As I opened my eyes, my mind was clear and my spirit rejuvenated. With a light heart, a heart full of surety and faith, I now live my life of prayer. God's light cured and healed my soul.

A New Life

The Jesus cure, the light of Christ shining within the soul, intensively leads to new life. The end result of all life's situations, all inner battles and conflicts with toxicity, is to be new life. Greater consciousness of the presence of the Risen Jesus and one's own unconscious attitudes and feelings, more and more highlights the life of the Christian who walks along the inner way.

The Gospel story of the ten virgins emphasizes the importance of readiness in living one's interior life with Christ. Jesus compared the kingdom of heaven to ten virgins who took their lamps and went out to meet the bridegroom. Five were foolish and five were wise. The foolish ones took no oil for their lamps. The wise ones took flasks of oil along with their lamps. When the bridegroom arrived, the foolish ones begged the wise ones to share their oil with them. The wise ones truthfully told them that they only had enough for themselves and encouraged the foolish ones to hurry and purchase their own oil.

No one can live out the inner way for another. No one can experience the Jesus cure for someone else. Each must walk his or her own way with Jesus into new life.

The five wise virgins left with the bridegroom. Sometime later, the five foolish virgins arrived at the wedding hall and begged the bridegroom to allow them to enter, but they were too late. Wisdom bids one to be always ready in the moment to receive the light of Christ.

The oil of readiness calls one forth to greater and greater consciousness of Christ Jesus within. To be ready, receptive at any moment in time, allows God's spirit and the human soul to freely mingle. Without this readiness, the grace of the moment can be missed. To be outside of Him leaves one with the sense of being left out in the cold. Our own lack of readiness, lacking the interior oil of ever present receptivity to God's spirit, makes for a heavy load, a depressed heart, and a toxic life. Light, known in the now, cures the soul and creates a vital sense of well-being: "So stay awake, because you do not know either the day or the hour" (Mt 25:13).

To Live You Must Die

Quite often I have encountered people longing to die. Life, they feel, has tossed too much their way. No longer do they greet each morning with expectation or anticipation of goodness; rather, every day brings with it an ominous feeling of dread and weighty concern.

The Jesus cure beckons the believer into fullness of life and out of daily dread. So easy is it to give lip service to the words of Jesus that He has come so that we might have life and life to the fullest. Have His words really taken hold in you! Have you been filled with His created life to such an extent that you now find life truly worth living?

Jesus proclaims, "I am the resurrection and the life." Jesus enlivens the soul, calling it out of the tomb of negative attitudes and moods. Jesus, known intimately and deeply, makes a difference in one's life.

Without Him, darkness, moodiness, and cynicism abound. With Him, an eagerness to live life fully floods the soul.

A Willing Death

Jesus' proclamation that He is the resurrection and the life confirms His uniqueness and individuality as the conveyer of all that is whole and holy. Standing apart from the mass psychology of the Judaism of His time, Jesus pointed out the way, the narrow path, to the Father. Jesus died to His own inclinations toward "falling in line," toward giving in to the pressures of the group movements of His day and age. Resurrection was the power and life lived within Him, and this reality He unwaveringly lived out and proclaimed.

To be no one but yourself is the ultimate objective of the Jesus cure. In so doing, you die to your own acquired false self. We all have developed ways of relating and manners of living that are at odds with our own true nature. Our innermost heart thrives on God-centered living that, quite often, has very little to do with fulfilling the expectations of the masses. Death, considered in these terms, allows the soul to gradually be free of pretentiousness and various falsities so that it might grow and develop in its own unique and creative way.

Resurrection power and life are maturing in everyone who knows the Jesus cure. Just as Jesus was His own person, so we remain more and more true to our own nature as Jesus touches and heals us. In the words of one ardent Christian, "I have never felt more fully myself than I do now as I have died to many of my old ways of living and relating to God."

Cardinal Newman eloquently wrote:

True Christians look just the same to the world as...the great mass of what are called respectable men...who in their hearts are very different; they make no great show, they go on in the same quiet, ordinary way as the others, but really they are training to be saints in Heaven. They do all they can to change themselves, to become like God, to obey God, to discipline themselves, to renounce the world; but they do it in secret, both because God tells them so to do and because they do not like it to be known.... True religion is a hidden light in the heart; and though it cannot exist without deeds, yet these are for the most part secret deeds, secret charities, secret prayers, secret self-denials, secret struggles, secret victories.... The holier a man is, the less he is understood by men of the world.

A Priest's Death

Father Christopher arrived for his first session with the following complaint: "I just want to die. I am tired of living and tired of my priesthood. At times I feel I cannot face another morning. Each day drags on with what seems to be unbearable burdens. I want to die."

His ostensibly suicidal thoughts concerned me. But as we talked further I understood them to represent his unconscious desire to end an old and destructive way of living. He had borne too much responsibility for things that were not his to bear. In his priesthood, his compulsion was to "make everything right for everybody." This needed to stop.

Father Christopher lived his life as everybody's "good guy." His parishioners thought of him as a model priest and certainly a living saint. He felt enamored by his own importance within the parish. In fact, for many years he thrived on people's admiration for him. After a while, however, the praises became heavy and burdensome, for with them came the obligation to always fulfill others' expectations.

After having served six years as a parish pastor, his vocation seemed dry and lifeless. His entire life lost any sense of meaning and purpose. Everyday he faced another day of pressure to fulfill everyone's expectations that he be "Father Good Guy" — the living saint.

It is no wonder that he felt like dying. Who would want to live under such circumstances? Through psychotherapy we gradually discovered that in actuality he did not really desire to commit suicide. Instead, his suicidal ideas symbolized his deep yearning to change, to die to an old way of life and give birth to a new one. His preoccupation with suicide faded away.

After approximately fourteen months of working together, definite life changes had occurred. He began to feel like he was more and more his own man. Rather than being at the beck and call of everyone's whims and fancies, he now steadied himself with confidence in his own feelings and discernment of God's leadings. Of course, this at first proved to be somewhat troublesome for him and the parish. The parishioners had lost "Father Good Guy." Their living saint was dead.

The real Father Christopher now lived. In reality, he was a very sensitive man, able to understand the needs of people, yet all the while able to maintain the integrity of his own character. No one pushed him around and he pushed no one around. Various parishioners attempted to pressure him to go back to being "Father Good Guy." He remained steadfast and assured them he understood their difficulty with him since he had changed, but he also assured them that with time and effort on both parts, an adjustment could be made. He demeaned neither himself nor them through this transition period.

As we neared the end of our work together, he shared:

> As I allowed grace to cure and heal me through the process of psychotherapy, I came to understand the meaning of real love. Real love, for me is taking responsibility for my life and letting others take responsibility for theirs. I encourage and support others in working out the burdens of their life, but I no longer take on their cares for them. I have my hands full with my own life. My ministry calls me to sensitively understand and encourage others on in their daily life with Christ. The best Christian witness I have to give is in living my own life freely and fully in Christ. The old "Father Good Guy" is dead — now, Father Christopher is alive.

Jesus and Jesus Only

The cultivation of one's own personality continues steadily on as toxic egocentricities are confronted, dealt with, and surrendered to the healing light of Jesus, and only to Jesus. In Him resides all that is whole and holy. A depth psychology that is Christian circumambulates around Jesus as the source of all that is whole and healing. This is not to denigrate other religious traditions. Indeed, religious bigotry must be carefully watched lest one fall into inflation and a hubris-caused limiting of God. Jesus, in all His fullness, touches hearts despite denominational or even religious preferences. He is love and light. All that finds its inspiration in love and light finds its inspiration in Jesus.

Thus for the Christian all identifications with psychological and theological founders and traditions must be eschewed. Freudianism, Jungianism, Thomism or any other -ism must be abandoned lest one lose centeredness in Christ. It is true that all the great theology and depth psychology traditions convey much truth. We must learn from all that is true and all that proclaims truth, all the while steadfastly remaining centered in the Risen Jesus.

This itself calls for death. To stand firmly rooted in the Christian tradition, while living and growing in the depths of the soul, happens only via grace. Burning rage can be felt from professional groups that demean the inner Christian way; the same blazing heat also flashes from the rigid churches which adamantly remain tied to conventional theologies propagating a very external form of religion. For the Christian who lives from soul neither professional identification nor church identification suffice or console. Only Jesus, and His interior call, can be heeded and followed.

As the unconscious is deeply plummeted, Jesus emerges in holiness and radiance. The deeper one travels into the unconscious, with light and truth as guides, the more profound becomes the inner experience of Jesus. The Jesus cure is, in all reality, the inner experience of Jesus.

Vanquishing Clouds of Confusion

The Jesus cure always imparts clarity of mind. A cloudy mind, a confused mind, steals away healthy living. It cripples the individual in relationships and in creative enterprises. Jesus, the Son of Righteousness with healing in His wings, shines into the darkened mind, parts the clouds of confusion, and restores clarity of attitude and feeling.

Jesus effects such a cure as the soul moves into Him. "For as the Father has life in himself, so He has granted the Son also to have life in himself" (Jn 5:26). The Father imparted life to Jesus as Jesus lived in the Father. As we move into greater centeredness in Jesus, He then imparts life and clarity, rather than confusion, to us.

Confusion, of course, can be expected at sometime or other by all of us. In fact, confusion frequently signals new life just ahead. Old ways of approaching life no longer seem to work. Old ways of solving problems lose their power. In essence, new growth can propel us into a temporary state of confusion while we await the realization of new insight and new personal development.

Thus, confusion cannot be escaped. We also cannot pull ourselves out of confusion. We can only pray for grace to see what we must see, grace that will see us through the confusion and into new life. Relief, release, and greater personal understanding accompany the journey from confusion into clarity of mind.

Chronic confusion, a state of affairs in which anxious thoughts almost constantly plague the mind, indicates that one may be holding on to egocentric and therefore toxic ways of living. This may involve inner attitudes or outer activities. The more one holds on to things that must be forsaken, the more confusion settles in. The only antidote to toxic confusion is understanding. Once one understands what new growth is expected of him or her, confusion abates and clear thinking emerges. To put off necessary life changes inflicts suffering, needless suffering, and intense confusion on the soul; to yield to the inevitable transformations of life gradually bears a fruitful harvest of settled and clear-minded attitudes and feelings.

Out of Confusion

Sonya, a woman of disciplined spiritual character, confessed her confusion regarding her own spiritual growth:

> As I continue in spiritual direction and prayer, I am concerned that I may outgrow my husband. He does not take to spiritual things very readily. Getting him to talk at all about his feelings or his relationship with God is practically impossible. If I continue to grow closer to God will that mean that we will end up in divorce?

Fortunately, I was acquainted with Sonya's husband. True, he was a man of minimal spiritual inclinations. But in no way could he be considered an anti-Christian or an anti-spiritual man. He was just more subtle and quieter in his way. I settled Sonya's confusion by offering her encouragement and heartfelt assurance that as she continued along her spiritual path, God would assuredly take care of her husband.

Approximately one year later I saw Sonya. She approached me after an evening conference and enthusiastically shared:

> You'll never guess what has happened between me and my husband. Not too long ago I dreamed that he was dead. Of course, the dream did not refer to his literal death, but rather to the fact that our old way of relating to each other, especially my way of relating to him, had died. As I have grown closer to Jesus, I am not only more at peace with myself but at peace with him. Now I see that in his own way he searches for God. I do not have to be his watch dog. He is growing and so am I. This I see clearly.

Sonya's insight discloses a very important message. Continuing to live in Him, to grow more centered in Jesus, leads one out of chaos and into clear-minded understanding. This sort of Jesus cure frees us up in our relations with others. It permits others to live their own life, all the while prompting us along our own individual way. In this we mature into a true relationship and intimacy that is characterized by greater consciousness and awareness of the presence of Jesus within.

Contemplation and Confusion

As Jesus has light in Himself, so that light is imparted to us as we contemplatively abide in Him. The key factor is to quietly enter into His presence, and therein discover greater centeredness and help.

Contemplative living often calls for intensive self-reflection. This is not to be confused with selfishness and egocentricity. Rather, true self-reflection is a deliberate pondering over one's life, a deliberation that leads to creativity and charity. Far from being morbidly introspective, the individual who daily engages in healthy self-reflection comes upon piercing self-revelations and more vivid experiences with God that eventually translate into charitable living with others. Ongoing contemplation nurtures this emotional and spiritual development so that life, in all its facets, becomes more lustrous and meaningful.

Henry, a fifty-one-year-old Roman Catholic, worried that entering into depth psychotherapy would threaten his Catholic faith. He obviously feared that continued analysis would analyze away his Catholic commitment. I assured him that the light-bearing process of psychotherapy never destroyed, but only built upon, the truth.

Much to his surprise, some three years later, his Roman Catholic faith had become more meaningful than ever. In fact, he had long contended with a highly conservative Cardinal who voiced hard line attitudes toward matters of faith and morals. Henry admitted that at times he could see no merit whatsoever in this high-ranking Cardinal.

Since intensive psychotherapy had sensitized him to truth, the realization of truth in all its vicissitudes, he more readily sensed the difference between authentic and fabricated spirituality. Near the ending of our treatment relationship, he recounted reading a beautiful passage on Christology. Henry felt inspiration and a greater love of God as the result of this literary work. He silently surmised that whoever wrote the passage surely knew and loved God. As he finished the work, his eyes came to the end of the page where the author's name was printed. There, as clear as could be, was the name of this archconservative Cardinal. Henry's soul witnessed the fact that the Holy Spirit works in and through not only the humble and unknown, but also through the mighty and powerful, as long as truth is humbly sought.

Without question, contemplation allows truth to surface, while an overly busy life clutters the soul and drowns out the voice of God. Confusion and disquietude creep in. Contemplation, spending time alone with God, centers one into the presence of the living Truth.

Burning Away Confusion

The Jesus cure inflames the soul with the love of God to such an extent that all toxic chaos and confusion is felt to be burned out of the mind. That is to say, anxious thoughts and worries give way to the Spirit of

Peace as the soul grows in self-understanding and the knowledge of God. This often requires intensity of work interiorly in terms of prayerful self-reflection and availability to the healing presence of God.

As purification from confusion takes place, the soul experiences great delight in life and in the love of God. Life takes on new meaning and freshness. The most mundane of tasks is now felt to be a gift to be done in the moment. All is done out of the love of God. Life itself feels enjoyable and delightful.

St. John of the Cross wrote of this purification:

> It will happen that while the soul is inflamed with the love of God, it will feel that a seraphim is assailing it by means of an arrow or dart which is all afire with love. And the seraphim pierces and cauterizes this soul which, like a red-hot coal, or better, a flame, is already enkindled. Where the soul is converted into the immense fire of love...
>
> O, happy wound, wrought by one who knows only how to heal! O, fortunate and choicest wound; you were made only for delight, and the quality of your affliction is delight and gratification for the wounded soul! You are great, O, delightful wound, because He who caused you is great! And your delight is great, because the fire of love is infinite and makes you delightful according to your capacity and greatness. O, then, delightful wound, so much more sublimely delightful, the more the cautery touches the intimate center of the substance of the soul, burning all that was burnable in order to give delight to all that could be delighted!

A Quiet Life — A Healed Life

Entering into the quiet, one enters into Jesus. The touch of the quiet is the touch of Jesus. God's nature, by its very aloneness, abides in quietness and tranquility. Only in peaceful settledness does the soul consciously know God.

So often we flee from the quiet. Quietness confronts us, face to face, with our own inner self. At times this proves to be a frightening experience. Especially for those who are caught up in busy living, solitude poses an extreme threat. Busyness often cloaks great interior conflict and storming. The rush of activity temporarily releases the nervous energy that results from living outside of God.

To live without being centered in Jesus allows one to escape facing his or her innermost feelings and attitudes. A superficial life of seeming ease and importance can dominate conscious activity. All the while, underneath, in the cauldrons of the unconscious is the storm of the unlived life; an unreflective personality is now dominated by misery and neuroses. When we run from quietness we end up running right into the arms of major unhappiness and toxic neuroses.

The Jesus cure, through steady self-reflection and prayerful silence, transforms a harried life into a quiet life. One who can be alone with himself or herself is one who can be alone with God. Jesus resides in the innermost place of the heart. His voice can be discerned only in the quiet. The hustle and bustle of life is, in fact, inevitable at times; but, it must not be allowed to be a constant. If nervous living characterizes one's life, then, in all likelihood, the distance between the soul and God has grown wide and deep. Only through reestablishing a prayerful vigilance and self-reflection will the soul come closer to Jesus and Jesus closer to the soul.

In reality, this interior way of quietness may prove quite disorienting. To truly follow Jesus calls for the relinquishment of old ways. In solitude, Jesus is encountered afresh, anew. This heightened awareness of Jesus must be paid for by wholehearted devotion and yielding to Him. Thomas Merton writes of the move into silence:

> The man who wants to deepen his existential awareness has to make a break with ordinary existence and this break is costly. It cannot be made without anguish and suffering. It implies loneliness and the disorientation of one who has to recognize that the old signposts don't show him the way and that, in fact, he has to find the way by himself without a map.

Tranquil Healing Streams

Often I have been puzzled by the fact that Psalm 23, so frequently recited during funerals, receives only infrequent attention as providing guidance for everyday life. The psalm begins with the acknowledgement that Yahweh is the Shepherd of the Soul. All interior needs and resulting external blessings are supplied by Him. In the words of the psalmist, "Yahweh is my shepherd, I lack nothing. In grassy meadows He lets me lie."

The way of Yahweh spawns tranquility. The psalmist confirms, "by tranquil streams He leads me to restore my spirit." In solitude and silence, with Yahweh and Yahweh alone as the center of one's life, the reality of the living water within is experienced. One close friend exclaimed, "At times in prayer, I feel the living waters flowing within me. My soul feels bathed in a luminous water of life. No longer dry and malcontent, I know tranquility and great peace of soul."

The restoration of spirit that accompanies quiet happens as the result of touching God. When one is alone, and enjoys aloneness, not as an escape but as a fulfillment, God is embraced. Holiness permeates such a time. The love of God, known firsthand during quietness and solitude, refreshes and heals the most battered heart.

In fact, interior discontent and malaise almost always indicate a need for solitude. Quite often we think that the reverse is true. I know of people who, when feeling badly, escape into the crowd, so to speak. They flee into one social activity after another. In a frenzy of nervous energy, they feel compelled to be with people. Inevitably, this exacerbates their anxiety. Distress of soul must be healed with quiet, not activity.

Too much socializing can destroy tranquility. One might feel quite peaceful and then find that an excess of social interactions has diluted inner quietude. Very few people live a quiet life or know the blessing of a quiet soul. Consequently, much socializing requires interchange with souls who themselves can be quite afflicted by their own noisy life. Too much of this superficial exchange tires even the most God-centered person.

The real challenge lies in remaining true to one's need for both inner tranquility and fruitful exchange with others. Remaining quiet within, all the while lovingly relating to significant others in your life, is the most mature way of living. It is the truest form of intimacy with others and with one's own soul. C. S. Lewis wrote of his fellow author, Charles Williams:

> The highest compliment I ever heard paid to them [Williams' manners] was by a nun. She said that Mr. Williams' manners implied a complete offer of intimacy without the slightest imposition of intimacy. He threw down all his barriers without ever implying that you should lower yours... He gave to every circle the whole man: all his attention, knowledge, courtesy, charity, were placed at your disposal.... This total offer of himself, but without that tacit claim which often accompanies such offers, made his friendship the least exacting in the world, and explains the surprising width of his contacts. One kept on discovering the most unlikely people loved him as well as we did.

The Cure and the Quiet

The psalmist continues, "Kindness and faithful love pursue me everyday of my life. I make my home in the house of Yahweh for all time to come" (Ps 23:6). Beside tranquil waters, the quietness of everyday living are kindness and faithfulness.

A kind man or woman radiates kindness as a matter of course in his or her life. Such a one lives with great interior tranquility. The dark one within has been faced and is being faced continually. This creates an inner resting place of peace since interiority is no longer adamantly resisted. Such a one has learned to be kind to his or her deepest self, to live in communion with his or her deepest self, and therefore can be kind to and live in communion with others.

Faithful love is the sister attitude of kindness. The adept in the interior way follows faithfully. He or she has come to know soul. Without question, the Jesus cure has bestowed incredible love for all that is human and holy. Faithful love extends to human relationships the experience of being understood without being intruded upon.

Kindness and faithful love emerge out of the quiet as cure continues. Throughout the course of life, kindness and faithful love increase as does interior union with God. Neither kindness nor faithful love come without time having been spent in quietness. It is quietness spent beside the streams of living water that bears the cure "everyday of my life."

Essentially, psychotherapy is a quieting process. A person learns to turn within and hear the voice of the quiet. Upon entering the consultation office, the patient begins to reveal all feelings, thoughts, memories, and dreams that come to mind, without blocking or censoring. In so doing, the quiet speaks. All that has been pained and wounded, all that has been neglected and driven away, rises from the depths. The psychotherapist remains quiet and listens, patiently realizing that the silence inevitably brings darkness into light.

This is not silence for silence's sake. Intuitive and empathic verbal exchanges must go on. However, they come as the result of listening and silence. They come only when the time is right. Neither speaking for speaking's sake or silence for silence's sake amounts to much. They both matter only in so far as they contribute to real listening and real understanding. The quiet, the cure, develops into life, the real living of daily life, in such a way that it becomes a sacrament in which Christ Himself is lived within, moves within, all the while consistently respecting the sacredness and uniqueness of the human personality.

Healing the personality through an experience of deep quiet often translates into greater physical health. I have worked with many cardiovascular and general medical patients. They often remark that a lack of quiet characterized their lifestyle prior to their ailment. Busyness and running from here to there plagued every waking moment, or so it seemed upon reflection. In the words of one candid soul, "I suffered from hurry sickness."

Illness forced many of them to slow down. A gentler and quieter existence soon became natural. Regular time for exercise, relaxation, and moderate work habits took the place of their former chronic frenzy. Quiet became a friend.

Many of them testified to the recuperative effects of quiet. High blood pressure decreased. Symptoms of anxiety abated. A general sense of well-being seemed to take hold. In all, quiet nurtured physical health.

The Jesus cure and quiet introduce subtle but definite physical and psychological transformations. The fullness of life carries with it the wonderful by-product of physical health. Not that we completely avoid all illness, but that its occurrence and impact are significantly decreased. As we live a human life, a very human life, health in mind, body, and spirit work together to usher us into more and more of the Divine Presence. To know Him in the quiet of the now is to know healing in the now.

Julian of Norwich wrote:

> Until I am really and truly one and
> fastened to God so that there is nothing
> created between us, I will never have
> full rest or complete happiness.
> For in order to love and have God who is
> uncreated, we must have knowledge of the
> smallest of creatures and empty ourselves
> of all that is created.
>
> We seek rest where there is no rest
> and therefore are uneasy.
>
> God is the True Rest
> Who wants to be known.
> God finds pleasure
> in being our true resting place.

The Way, The Truth, The Life

In utter quietness and stillness Jesus speaks to the soul: "I am the Way; I am Truth and Life." To know the Jesus cure places one in a face-to-face encounter with Him who is the Way, the Truth, and the Life. Jesus is all three. Not one can be forgotten. He is the only way to the Father, the spoken truth of the Father, and the life of the Father.

The Way

As the only way to the Father, Jesus stirs deeply within the heart of every man and woman. Anyone who has felt holiness and wholeness has felt Jesus. Despite formal declarations of faith or lack thereof, Jesus can and will touch and transform, cure, the soul. A Buddhist, an agnostic, a Hindu, a Protestant, or Catholic who has encountered the Holy, the Sacred, has encountered the reality of the Risen Jesus. He is the Way, the only Way.

In private psychotherapy practice, I work with many professing Christians. However, I have discovered that often their external perspective with regard to faith can interfere with the journey of their soul toward God. Long held perspectives and outmoded beliefs can threaten to thwart the soul's development. Many have painfully recorded, "I am so afraid to continue growing. I feel that I have become different than everyone else who goes to my church. I don't see God in the same way anymore. I am afraid that if I continue growing, I will become too different from them. They might reject and ostracize me."

Inevitably, such a one discovers that Jesus and only Jesus is the Way. Rigid church rituals and ways of worship cannot replace the individual's personal experience of Jesus. Quite often this alters one's relationship with the institutional church and perhaps even with fellow believers. However, with time and continued inner development, this problem usually takes care of itself. The loss of certain types of friends and relationships opens the way for the establishment of newer and deeper friendships based on more genuine living.

Toward the end of her analysis, one patient remarked:

> I felt so disoriented for the longest time. Old friendships that had been based on superficialities and neurotic clinging got swept away. I felt so alone for the longest time. Although, I do have to admit that I never really felt lonely even though I was alone. I drew much consolation from a feeling of being healthier. Now, as a

matter of course, I am involved with others who desire to live their lives genuinely centered in Jesus. These people are real people, with real hurts and pains in their lives, and with a sincere openness to truth.

The Truth

Jesus Himself is Truth; therefore, those who follow Him must also be truth. Each moment of living brings a new opportunity to know truth. To maintain the status quo, assuming that one is always truthful, is to lapse into supreme dishonesty. Real truth requires vigilance and the realization that we all maintain the capacity for dishonesty and betrayal.

At the Last Supper Jesus offered Judas a singular grace that could have inspired him into truth. As Jesus dipped the bread into the wine and offered it to Judas, He passed on grace. Jesus offered Himself, the Truth, to Judas. I imagine that Jesus looked straight into the eyes of Judas as he swallowed the bread moments before making his decision to betray Jesus. While Judas placed the bread in his mouth, chewed, and swallowed, Jesus waited for his decision.

Previous scriptures record that Jesus knew the heart of man; He could read the heart of Judas. Even with Eucharistic grace, Judas opted for dishonesty and betrayal. Jesus knew his thoughts and, without Judas speaking a word, Jesus dismissed him to do what he had to do.

Judas is not alone in his betrayal of Jesus. All of us have countered the truth at some point in our lives. Daily, each moment, the decision for truth stands before us.

So difficult is the process of truth. It is ongoing, never ending. If it were easy, everyone would follow the Way of truth. But, the Way is narrow.

Just this week, the healing reality of truth seared my consciousness anew. A patient stood on the verge of killing himself. In a flash of mere moments, he felt the impulse to slash his wrists and his neck. This was no superficial threat. Death called out to him as a seductive mistress.

For him the decision was clear: truth or toxic untruth, life or death, healing or disintegration. Sharp razors were on the counter before him. He had slashed his wrists before. He knew how to do it. In just a few minutes it could all be over. He could be dead.

He recounted this nightmarish temptation during our next session. In his mind, slashing himself, committing suicide, meant not having to face the truth with me. His darkest secrets would never be exposed to the light of our relationship and the healing light of Christ. He could hide, perhaps forever. It seemed like a way out, an easy way out, a way out from the truth.

But he was unsure of death. The truth could follow him to the other side. Maybe there was no way out of having to deal with truth. At least he knew what he was in for — somewhat — with me. He was unsure and quite frightened about what might happen to him in death. He opted to live, to face truth, to find healing no matter what.

The Life

To be infused with life is inevitable for the believer. One who believes, who wholeheartedly follows the way and the truth, unquestionably encounters infusions of awesome life. God is the giver of life and all who seek Him are transformed into life.

Nikos Kazantzakis's novel *St. Francis* has Brother Leo recalling the mystical encounter of St. Francis with the unrelenting Source of Life:

> The three days came to an end....I felt delighted...but I was trembling at the thought of seeing Francis. To talk three days with the Almighty was to expose yourself to immense danger. God might hurl you into a terrible chasm where He was able to survive but a man was not.... Francis suddenly emerged from the cave. He was radiant — a gleaming cinder. "Well, Brother Leo, are you ready?... Have you donned your warlike armor?"...He seemed delirious. His eyes were inflamed.... I was terrified. Could he have taken leave of his senses? He understood and laughed, but his fire did not subside. "People have enumerated many terms of praise for the Lord up to now...but I shall enumerate still more. Listen to what I shall call Him: The Bottomless Abyss, the Insatiable, the Merciless, the Indefatigable, the Unsatisfied. He who never wants said to poor, unfortunate mankind 'enough!'" Coming still closer he placed his lips next to my ear and cried in a thunderous voice, "Not enough!...If you ask, Brother Leo, that God command without respite, I can tell you, for I learned it these past three days and nights in the cave. Listen! Not enough! Not enough! 'I can't go further,' whines man. 'You can,' the Lord replies. 'I shall break in two,' Man whines again. 'Break!' the Lord replies." Francis' voice had begun to crack. I became angry.... "What more does He expect from you?" I asked. "Didn't you restore San Dominanos?" "Not enough!" "Well, what more does He expect?" "I asked Him, Brother Leo....He answered, 'Go to My Church, the Portincula. I shall tell you there.' So, Brother Leo, let's go down and see what

> He wants. Cross yourself, tighten the rope around your waist.
> We're dealing with God and from Him there is no escape."

For the believer there is no escape from the awesome journey of being transformed into life. God demands it. He wants all of us, no partial faith commitment, no holding back even a little. He wants all of our life and for us to have all of His love and life. In consulting with the mother superior of a large religious order, the choice between death and life for the monastery community became quite obvious. The superior alarmingly confided, "The devil is in our monastery." Somehow, in some way, evil, decided in willful unconsciousness, had crept into the monastery's inner sanctum.

She related a dream in which she had spotted a black widow crawling through the monastery halls. No one else in the community was able to see the spider. As she approached the black widow, she heard a voice instructing her, "Have nothing to do with the black widow or you and your monastery will die."

She awoke from this nightmare in a cold sweat. We came to understand that the situation was indeed serious and even perilous. For many months community members had been irritable with one another. Some sisters would not speak with other sisters. Anger and frustration ran rampant in the monastery.

As we explored the image of the black widow, one particular nun in the community came to mind. She collected spiders. It was her hobby. She had been with the monastery, on sabbatical from her teaching assignment, for approximately twelve months. This was approximately when the torment entered the monastery.

Upon reflection, the superior admitted her concern with regard to this nun: "She talks about sisters behind their backs. She sets sister against sister. She is extremely divisive."

We had found our toxic black widow. The mother superior asked, "But shouldn't we befriend her and try and help her through her problem?" I reiterated:

> You must be careful. God's voice stated plainly to have nothing to
> do with her. You must let her leave the monastery when her
> sabbatical is over. Do not renew her stay. If you do befriend her,
> Mother, you and other members of your community will suffer a
> potentially lethal spiritual blow. This nun is quite unconscious,
> willfully so, and therefore dangerous.

Three months after the "black widow nun" left, complete harmony was restored to the monastery. Life calls for consciousness. Consciousness means facing intrapsychic deceit and interpersonal darkness. At times cuts must be made, for the sake of life and health. "...And from Him there is no escape."

Seven

The Healing of Toxicity:
Body, Mind, and Soul

Once again, religious toxicity refers to that psychological state of ill health in which individual growth and development is thwarted by religious expectations, legalities, and attitudes. Although the person may appear to be quite "Christian," such a one is interiorly plagued by a vague unhappiness, lack of fulfillment, and even misery. Toxicity causes a spiritual climate of immaturity and oppression.

The purpose of organized religion is to further the maturing process of the individual soul. The institution is present for the individual, not the individual for the institution. Strong and healthy individuals help to create a healthy sense of community and make for a soundly managed church. Institutional domination and control by "the powers that be" always signals an unhealthy organization composed of insecure and toxic people who demand blind obedience and subservience to the legalistic norms of the religious enterprise. The healthy individual quietly leaves control-minded people, parishes, and churches, lest toxicity be encouraged or incurred.

Once toxicity infects the body, mind, and/or soul, deep healing must be sought. With patience and perseverance, and a careful willingness to painstakingly face truth, one can undergo interior healing that will create a life of well-being and creativity. To be cleansed of toxicity means to enter into the deep unconscious. In our innermost depths God's healing grace abounds: "Deep is calling to deep by the roar of your cataracts, all your waves and breakers have rolled over me...my Savior, my God" (Ps 43:7, 11).

Deep Bodily Healing

Psychological toxicity may create bodily dysfunction and disease. With individual growth thwarted, one's body may react quite negatively and painfully. An interior dis-ease potentiates a bodily disease.

When one's emotions are upheaved, one's spiritual life contaminated by conflict and despair, it only makes sense that the body will also suffer. Physical health and well-being coincide greatly with interior health and well-being. A healthy mind and soul make for a healthy body, and a healthy body can contribute to health of mind and soul.

In particular, two facets of psychological phenomena create health or disease in one's life. Toxic attitudes and toxic relationships act to affect personal well-being. Attitudes are toxic, unhealthy, for the body whenever the physical, the sensual, and overall health are impugned. Relationships become toxic for the body whenever one person attempts to control, manipulate, and/or dominate another via sickness or threats of sickness. Thus, attitudes and relationships decidedly influence physical health toward toxicity and sickness, or toward health and well-being.

Toxic Attitudes and Sickness

Richard, a very pious and devout Catholic, felt convinced that sickness drew him closer to God. He sought out ill health. He thought that the more he suffered the more Christ-like he would become. Sickness, then, became a means of drawing closer to God — or so he thought.

From colds to the flu, to various gastrointestinal and bronchial disorders, he suffered. With each sickness came the intense conviction that holiness was close at hand. He viewed ill health as God-given and grace-filled.

Clinically, Richard was quite morose and depressed. His sad state psychologically betrayed a deep inner disorder relating to various long-held religious attitudes. In his mind, the body counted for nothing at all save to be whipped and beat into subjugation by the spirit. This old, worn-out Catholic attitude left him quite miserable, depressed, and spiritually thwarted.

During his course in long-term, in-depth psychotherapy, the falsity of his religiosity became apparent. His dreams manifested the symbol of a sickly, tired-out old Catholic priest who was rigidly tied into pre–Vatican II medieval theology in which the body was seen as evil and to be despised for the sake of spiritual growth. The dream depicted the priest as negative, destructive, and near death.

Fortunately, Richard was able to work through the toxic religiosity that condemned healthy, human vitality. His old, medieval religious attitude toward the body died. In its place grew a healthy respect for his humanity, sensuality, and physical vigor. Rather than moping in sickness, he now exercised regularly, ate healthy food, and developed a new religious perspective. Richard realized that a healthy body developed out of a healthy sense of self and a healthy relationship with God.

Along with attitudes, relationships may also exert a toxic effect on the body. Mixing with people who attempt to control, dominate, or manipulate us, especially on religious grounds, can create or magnify sickness. What is bad for the individual is bad for the body. Sick relationships can make for a sick body.

Tom was constantly warned by his mother that he was a fragile and sickly young man. His mother was a very "committed Christian." She often related that her sensitivity for him was founded on love. She did not want him to suffer from asthma and related difficulties that "might even kill him" if she did not take care of him.

She frequently commented, "Stay close to me, Tom, and I'll take care of you. I feel that it's my special place in your life to make sure that you are as healthy as possible. I'm always here for you, Tom."

Prior to Tom's leaving home for college, his mother insisted, "Now don't go out for soccer and other sports, especially track. Your asthma always acts up and I won't be able to be by your side. Don't do too much there at the college or else you'll get sick."

When Tom questioned me about his mother's concern, I reflected that he obviously felt quite oppressed and controlled by her. He had a decision to make. He could either remain true to her advice and therefore controlled, even at a distance, by his mother; or he could leave for college and begin making his own decisions. The choice was his.

The year away from his mother proved fruitful for Tom. He decided to engage in athletics, especially since his medical doctor had not warned him to the contrary. In fact, his physician said that he had the stamina and strength to participate in whatever sport appealed to him. Tom remained symptom free until the end of the school year when he arrived back at his mother's home for the summer. The first day back he suffered a severe asthma attack.

Once we talked, Tom understood that his mother would never change. Despite her conscious love and concern, her true attitude toward Tom was one of control and subjugation. Under the Christian pretext of caring, she exerted an unconscious and powerful domination over Tom. She was, in fact, toxic for him.

Tom decided to return to the college for summer courses. He discovered that visiting his mother for no longer than three days at a time was all he could do without becoming ill again. The intense toxicity in their relationship called for an appropriate distance and minimal contact between them. This sufficed to ensure Tom's continued growth and well-being as an individual.

At times distancing oneself from the toxic relationship is required for the sake of health. Sometimes a complete end to the relationship may be necessary. At other times the other party is willing and able to grow in consciousness, change, and permit the development of a healthy relationship; this is ideal, but unfortunately all too often this does not occur. Consciousness, health, and a hearty individuation are the mainstays of the life of the soul, meaning that all that interferes, including toxic relationships, must be forsaken so as to grow in personal and interpersonal well-being.

Prayer for Healing

This prayer for healing can help you to settle into your soul so that the process of deep bodily healing might begin. It is a beginning — only a beginning. Deep quietude helps us to realize what we must realize. Inner quietude helps us to face truth. Deep prayer, of the kind you are about to experience, can facilitate consciousness — an understanding that an inner conflict, an inner toxicity, may be causing bodily discomfort and, perhaps, disease.

Sit quietly in a comfortable chair...slowly close your eyes...listen to the sounds in the room...become aware of the feeling of the air on your skin...even be aware of your body breathing, inhaling and exhaling. Allow your body to breath very gently and naturally on its own. Slowly and gently your body inhales and exhales, rhythmically and naturally...as you inhale, very gently focus on the word "Lord"...as you exhale, very gently focus on the word "Jesus." "Lord" as you inhale. "Jesus" as you exhale. "Lord" as you inhale. "Jesus" as you exhale. Continue this very gentle prayer of focusing on the name of Jesus. For five minutes allow yourself to gently focus on His name.

...At the end of your five minutes become aware of where your body is hurting or ailing. With your eyes closed, sense the warmth of God's healing touch in that area of your body. Allow the warmth of healing grace to settle into your body.

...Also become aware of what has been troubling you the most in your personal life. Conflict of this sort can in some instances cause ailments or impede the process of healing. As this conflict comes to mind, very gently continue focusing on the name of Jesus and sensing

the warmth of healing grace in your body, especially in the area where
you are ailing or hurting.

Once you are ready, after approximately five minutes in total for
this prayer, slowly and gently open your eyes feeling relaxed and re-
freshed. Relaxed and refreshed.

I would encourage you to practice this prayer every day for a period
of one month. Depending on the exact nature of the physical problem,
some individuals may experience relief, others may discover that they
now feel a greater sense of assurance in seeking deeper health. Quality
medical care and the consideration of in-depth psychotherapy may
be warranted if the symptoms are unremitting. Sound spirituality and
medical treatment always work together to provide healing grace.
All healing comes from God, whether felt directly via prayer or through
the care of a qualified doctor — or both. All deep bodily healing comes
from God.

Deep Mental Healing

Toxicity also potentially infects the mind. One's thoughts and attitudes
can be severely disrupted by religious toxicity. When this happens, one
not infrequently loses zest for living. The thought, "life is not worth
living" can consciously or unconsciously possess an individual.

Once again, both interior attitudes and external relationships create
the host for religious toxicity to feed on the mind. Toxic attitudes and
toxic relationships of a religious nature breed mental distress. James
repeatedly complained that he did not know why he suffered from such
miserable depression on Sundays. On no other day of the week did he
feel so disabled and depressed. As we investigated the matter further, the
cause of his toxic depression soon became apparent. Every Sunday, he
felt forced to attend Mass in his parish, a Mass that was said by a very
negative, demeaning, and judgmental priest. The pastor would rant and
rave at the parishioners during his homily. A more oppressive and
negative Sunday liturgy one could not imagine.

James reported the following dream in his psychotherapy session:

> I was seated for Sunday Mass in the same pew in which I usually sit
> with my family. Father yelled out my name from the pulpit. I
> remember his finger pointing at me, making me feel as though I
> was a miserable worm. He made me bow down in front of him in

order to receive communion. I awoke from this dream shaking and
trembling from being exposed to the control and fury of Father.

As we explored the matter, it became clear that James needed to
consider leaving his parish. The pastor had been confronted by a number
of parishioners and asked to tone down and consider a more positive
approach. Father quickly lambasted and publicly derided such parishioners. The only alternative for James was to leave the parish.

The same week that he left the parish he discovered that the old
feelings of toxic depression subsided. Exposure to a toxic priest filled
with toxic attitudes was more than he or any of his fellow parishioners
could bear. James and a number of other truthful parishioners joined
another parish that was more life-giving in its approach. In this case, a
toxic relationship filled with toxic attitudes created a mental state for
James such that he no longer felt like living. Leaving the toxic
environment helped to initiate deep healing in his mind. James realized
that life was indeed worth living.

Healing Prayer

As we together pray for deep mental healing, consider that the actual
process of depth work takes patience and time. Our prayer together helps
to set the healing process in motion or to facilitate a process that has
already been initiated. Prayer of this sort, or indeed any prayer, is not the
end all. Prayer, at its best, opens the soul to an infusion of grace. Prayer
readies the soul for deep mental healing.

*Now, let us pray quietly and deliberately. Be seated in a comfortable
position. Slowly close your eyes. Become aware of the sounds in the
room, the feeling of the air on your skin, and the natural process of
inhaling and exhaling. Become aware that this is a time to relax deeply
and enter into God's presence.*

*Very gently as you inhale, focus on "Lord," and as you exhale,
gently focus on "Jesus." Very rhythmically and slowly inhaling "Lord"
and exhaling "Jesus." For the next two to three minutes allow yourself
to gently focus on the name of Jesus paired with your inhaling and
exhaling. Allow the name of Jesus to relax you and deepen your felt
experience of God's peace.*

*Slowly become aware of the dark attitude of lethargy, tiredness, and
negativism that has overtaken you. The mental outlook that "life is not*

*worth living" may have temporarily injured you. Become aware of this
dark attitude.*

*Gradually become aware of the presence of Jesus within you and
surrounding you. Realize that Jesus speaks to you this moment: "I have
come that you might have life and life abundantly. I have come that you
might have life and life abundantly. I have come that you might have
life and life abundantly."*

*Reflect on the life-giving words of Jesus that life can be yours in
abundance, that LIFE IS WORTH LIVING. Reflect on this in your mind
and repeat it once again mentally. LIFE IS WORTH LIVING. Once
again, LIFE IS WORTH LIVING. Continue to reflect on these words
until you sense their meaning filling you and stirring within you.*

*Once you are ready, very slowly and very gently open your eyes
feeling relaxed, refreshed, and rejuvenated. One more time, with your
eyes open, slowly reflect on the message, LIFE IS WORTH LIVING.*

This healing prayer can help you to further the life-giving
realization that real life is not meant to be filled with despair and
hopelessness. Such a dark attitude and mood is a symptom of mental
toxicity that needs to be worked out of one's system. Prayer, spiritual
direction, and psychotherapy all work together to enable the sufferer to
discover release, freedom, and fullness of life.

Deep Soul Healing

Finally, toxicity may infect the soul. Interpersonal and attitudinal
poisons may launch themselves into the deepest recesses of one's
innermost being. With toxicity of soul, the individual finds himself or
herself in dire straits, loaded down with misery.

Dreams are of pre-eminent help in diagnosing toxicity of soul.
Dream symbols and metaphors of sickness, disease, filth, and infection
may indicate a state of interior toxicity. Disease-spreading insects and
vermin such as cockroaches and rats also suggest a present or impending
toxicity. Dreams attempt to raise one's consciousness to the clear-
minded perception of such spiritual sickness.

The manifestation of toxicity in the soul via dreams denotes a very
serious condition of internal distress that may be remedied only via
intensive spiritual direction and/or in-depth psychotherapy. Frequently
both are required. Postponing the working through of toxicity sets up a

potentially hazardous state of affairs. The person may indeed go from bad to worse or, more tragically, may completely anesthetize feelings of misery and malcontent, and go on to believe that all is well when in fact he or she has become an unfeeling and emotionally rigid person having now joined the population of the living dead.

Those who humbly and openly enter into deep psychotherapy are not only motivated by pain but also by a desire to discover truth. The painstaking and patient integration of truth via psychotherapy not only works through internal toxicity but also develops a more clearly defined sense of self. Only then does the Christian begin to experience the fullness of the reality that one's innermost self is created in the image and likeness of God, created to live a good and creative life, to live a life deeply felt from the soul wherein resides the presence of the Risen Jesus.

I encourage you to discern the presence of toxicity in your life, especially when it is veiled with religious attitudes. To confront toxicity means to be willing to risk change. A change in one's long-held, but growth-thwarting, attitudes and relationships requires deep courage. Movement through and away from toxicity and into health can indeed be, at one and the same time, relieving and frightening. Old ways are familiar and well-worn ways. New ways of grace-filled living seem promising, but, you may ask yourself, do you have what it takes to initiate the journey toward individuation and healing from toxicity? I believe you do. Allow me to conclude with a story:

> As the story goes, twin boys were conceived in the womb of their mother. As time went on they grew and developed. Soon they happily conversed: "It feels wonderful to be alive, so good to be here together!"
>
> The twins explored the world of the womb in which they lived. Mysteriously they discovered that their mother's cord transmitted life to them. They exclaimed: "Our mother's love comes to us, for she shares her own life with us."
>
> As the months moved forward, the twins realized that they were changing. One of them inquired, "Why do we change so? What is the meaning of this?" The other replied, "Soon the world of our mother's womb, the world that we know, will come to an end." The first one in a frightened voice exclaimed, "I don't want this to end. I don't want to leave here. I want to always be here." The other twin answered, "We have no choice. We must go on. But, perhaps there is life after birth." The frightened one countered, "But how can that be? Once the life cord to our mother is cut, how can life be possible? Remember, we know that others

were here in the womb before us and no one of them has ever returned here to tell us that there is life after birth. No, all is lost, this has to be the end."

The forlorn twin despairingly continued, "All of our time in the womb has been for nought. It has been meaningless. Maybe our mother does not exist at all." The other twin asserted, "Our mother has to be real! Or else, how did we get here? How do we stay alive?"

The tormented twin stumbled on, "But have you ever seen our mother? Maybe she just lives in our imagination. Maybe we just made her up in order to make ourselves feel good."

The last days of the twins in the womb were days of confusion, doubt, fear. At last, the moment of birth arrived.

When the twins passed on from the world of the womb their eyes were opened. They wept. Now they could see... and what they saw exceeded their fondest dreams.

> What no eye has seen
> And no ear has heard,
> What the mind of man
> Cannot visualize;
> All that, God has prepared
> For those who love Him. (1 Cor 2:9)

Bibliography

Athanasius, Saint. *Life of Anthony.* In *Post-Nicene Fathers.* Second Series, Vol. 4. Grand Rapids: Eerdmans, 1957.

Chariton, Igumen. *The Art of Prayer: An Orthodox Anthology.* Translated by E. Kadloubovsky and E. M. Palmer. London: Faber and Faber, 1966.

de Mello, Anthony. *Taking Flight.* New York: Doubleday, 1988.

Doyle, Brendan. *Meditations of Julian of Norwich.* Santa Fe, N.M.: Bear & Co., 1983.

Elliot, T. S. *The Waste Land.* Edited and with an introduction by Valerie Elliot. New York: Harcourt Brace Jovanovich, 1971.

James, William. *The Varieties of Religious Experience.* Cambridge, Mass.: Harvard University Press, 1985.

John of the Cross, Saint. *The Collected Works of Saint John of the Cross.* Translated by Kieran Kavanaugh, O.C.D., and Otilio Rodriguez, O.C.D. Washington, D.C.: Institute of Carmelite Studies, 1979.

Jones, L. Alan. *Soul Making.* New York: Harper and Row, 1985.

Jung, C. G. *Collected Works.* Bollingen Series XX, ed. Sir Herbert Read, Michael Fordham, and Gerhard Adler. Translated by R. F. C. Hull. Vol. 8, *The Structure and Dynamics of the Psyche.* Princeton University Press.

Justice, Blair. *Who Gets Sick — Thinking and Health.* Houston: Peak Press, 1987.

Kazantzakis, Nikos. *St. Francis.* New York: Simon & Schuster, 1962.

Lewis, C. S. *Essays Presented to Charles Williams*. Oxford: Oxford University Press, 1947.

Merton, Thomas. *Contemplation in a World of Action*. New York: Doubleday, 1971.

Nomura, Yushi. *Desert Wisdom: Sayings From the Desert Fathers*. New York: Image Books, 1984.

Padus, Emrika. *The Complete Guide to Your Emotions and Your Health*. Emmaus, Penn.: Rodale Press, 1986.

Psychology Today. "Men Without Passion," December, 1988.

Reinhold, H. A., ed. *The Soul Afire*. Garden City, N. Y.: Image Books, 1973.

Symeon, Saint. *The New Theologian: Hymns of Divine Love*. Translated by George A. Maloney, S. J. Denville, N.J.: Dimension Books, 1975.

The Way of the Pilgrim. Translated by R. N. French. New York: The Seabury Press, 1965.